INSPIRE MATHS

PUPIL TEXTBOOK 2A

Consultant and author
Dr Fong Ho Kheong

Authors
Chelvi Ramakrishnan and Michelle Choo

UK consultants
Carole Skinner, Simon d'Angelo and Elizabeth Gibbs

Introduction

Inspire Maths is a comprehensive, activity-based programme designed to provide pupils with a firm foundation in maths and to develop the creative and critical thinking skills to become fluent problem solvers.

Inspire Maths makes learning maths fun and rewarding through the use of engaging illustrations and games that help to reinforce and consolidate learning.

For the teacher:

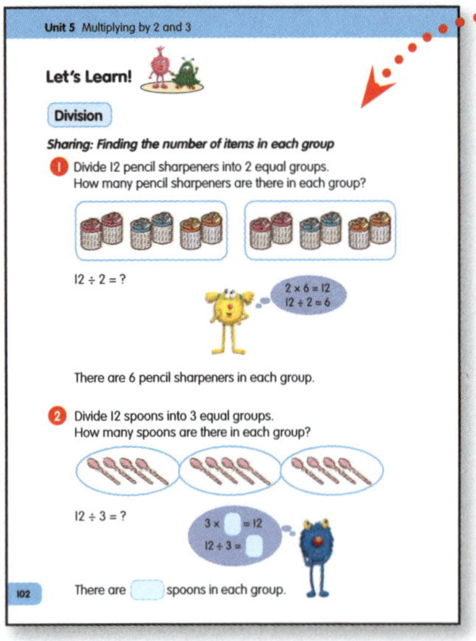
Unit 5 Multiplying by 2 and 3

Let's Learn!

Division

Sharing: Finding the number of items in each group

1. Divide 12 pencil sharpeners into 2 equal groups.
How many pencil sharpeners are there in each group?

12 ÷ 2 = ?

2 × 6 = 12
12 ÷ 2 = 6

There are 6 pencil sharpeners in each group.

2. Divide 12 spoons into 3 equal groups.
How many spoons are there in each group?

12 ÷ 3 = ?

3 × ☐ = 12
12 ÷ 3 = ☐

There are ☐ spoons in each group.

102

Use the engaging and highly scaffolded **Let's Learn!** to introduce concepts. Integrated questions allow for immediate assessment and consolidation of concepts learnt.

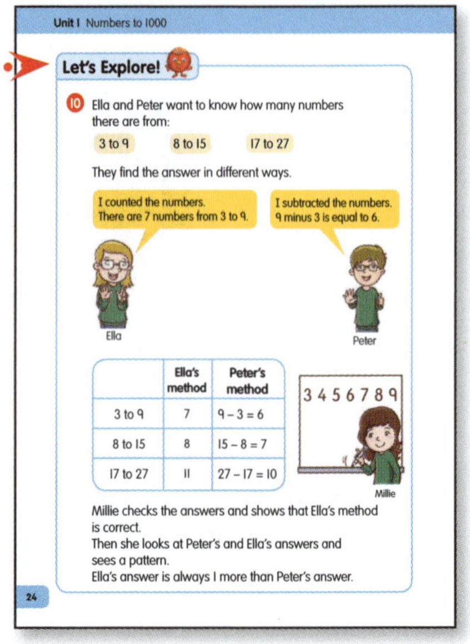
Unit 1 Numbers to 1000

Let's Explore!

10. Ella and Peter want to know how many numbers there are from:

3 to 9   8 to 15   17 to 27

They find the answer in different ways.

	Ella's method	Peter's method
3 to 9	7	9 − 3 = 6
8 to 15	8	15 − 8 = 7
17 to 27	11	27 − 17 = 10

Millie checks the answers and shows that Ella's method is correct.
Then she looks at Peter's and Ella's answers and sees a pattern.
Ella's answer is always 1 more than Peter's answer.

24

Carry out investigative activities in **Let's Explore!** These allow pupils to apply concepts learnt.

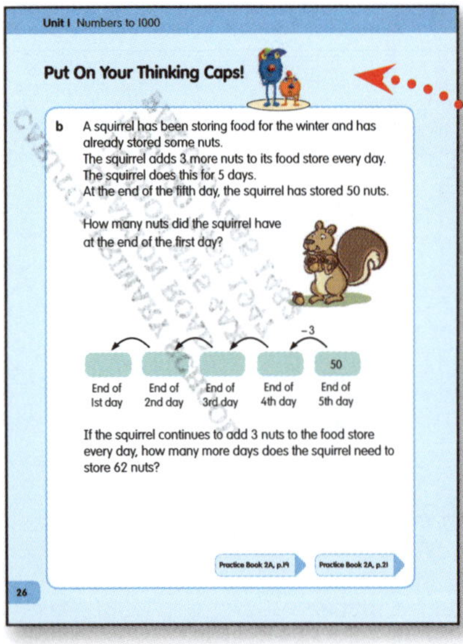
Unit 1 Numbers to 1000

Put On Your Thinking Caps!

b. A squirrel has been storing food for the winter and has already stored some nuts.
The squirrel adds 3 more nuts to its food store every day.
The squirrel does this for 5 days.
At the end of the fifth day, the squirrel has stored 50 nuts.

How many nuts did the squirrel have at the end of the first day?

If the squirrel continues to add 3 nuts to the food store every day, how many more days does the squirrel need to store 62 nuts?

Practice Book 2A, p.19   Practice Book 2A, p.21

26

Challenge pupils to solve non-routine questions by applying relevant heuristics and thinking skills in **Put On Your Thinking Caps!**

For the parent/guardian:

Home Maths

Build home-school links and make maths come alive by using the tips in Home Maths to help children apply mathematical concepts to daily life.

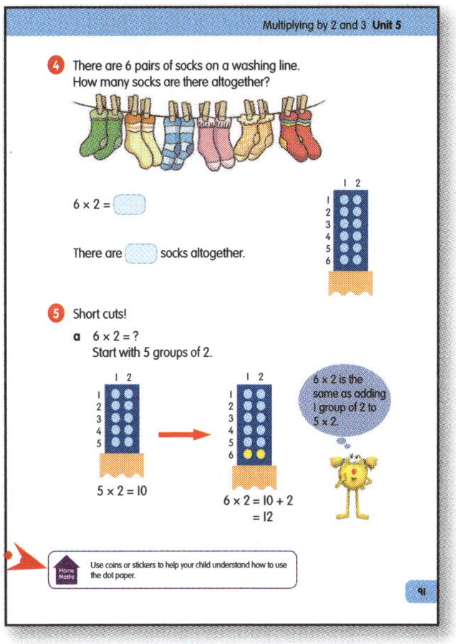
Multiplying by 2 and 3 **Unit 5**

4 There are 6 pairs of socks on a washing line.
How many socks are there altogether?

6 × 2 = ☐

There are ☐ socks altogether.

5 Short cuts!

a 6 × 2 = ?
Start with 5 groups of 2.

5 × 2 = 10

6 × 2 = 10 + 2
= 12

Use coins or stickers to help your child understand how to use the dot paper.

91

For the pupil:

Enjoy **Inspire Maths** with your friends. Explore your learning through activities and games.

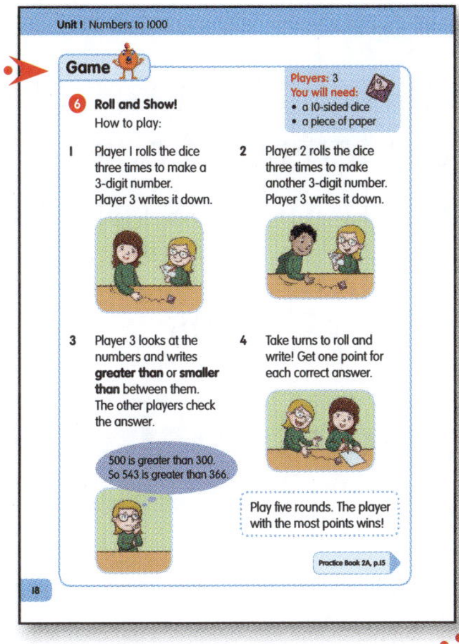
Unit 1 Numbers to 1000

Game

6 **Roll and Show!**

How to play:

Players: 3
You will need:
- a 10-sided dice
- a piece of paper

1 Player 1 rolls the dice three times to make a 3-digit number.
Player 3 writes it down.

2 Player 2 rolls the dice three times to make another 3-digit number.
Player 3 writes it down.

3 Player 3 looks at the numbers and writes **greater than** or **smaller than** between them.
The other players check the answer.

4 Take turns to roll and write! Get one point for each correct answer.

Play five rounds. The player with the most points wins!

Practice Book 2A, p.15

18

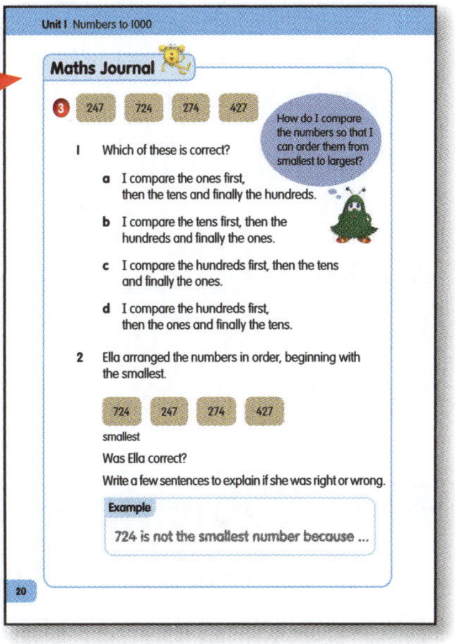
Unit 1 Numbers to 1000

Maths Journal

3 247 724 274 427

1 Which of these is correct?

a I compare the ones first, then the tens and finally the hundreds.

b I compare the tens first, then the hundreds and finally the ones.

c I compare the hundreds first, then the tens and finally the ones.

d I compare the hundreds first, then the ones and finally the tens.

2 Ella arranged the numbers in order, beginning with the smallest.

724 247 274 427
smallest

Was Ella correct?

Write a few sentences to explain if she was right or wrong.

Example

724 is not the smallest number because ...

20

Share what you have learnt, create your own questions and become aware of your own mathematical thinking in your **Maths Journal**.

Contents

Unit 1 Numbers to 1000

Let's Learn!

Counting

1 Put 10 together to make .

Then put together 10 .

10 tens = 100

100

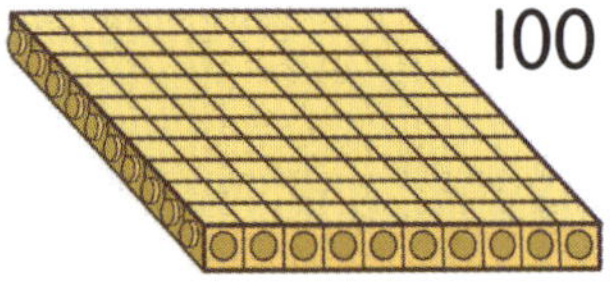

108

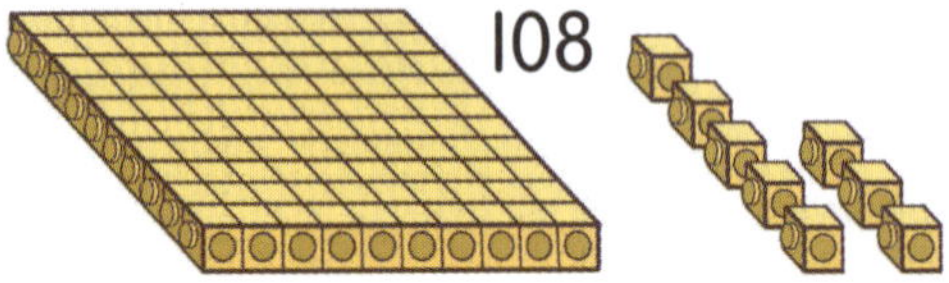

2 352

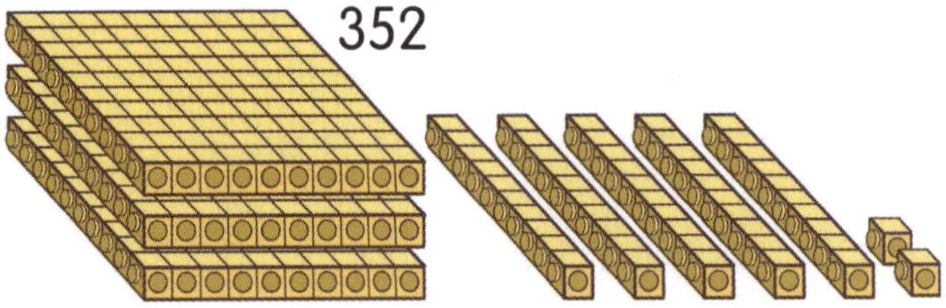

3 How many are there?

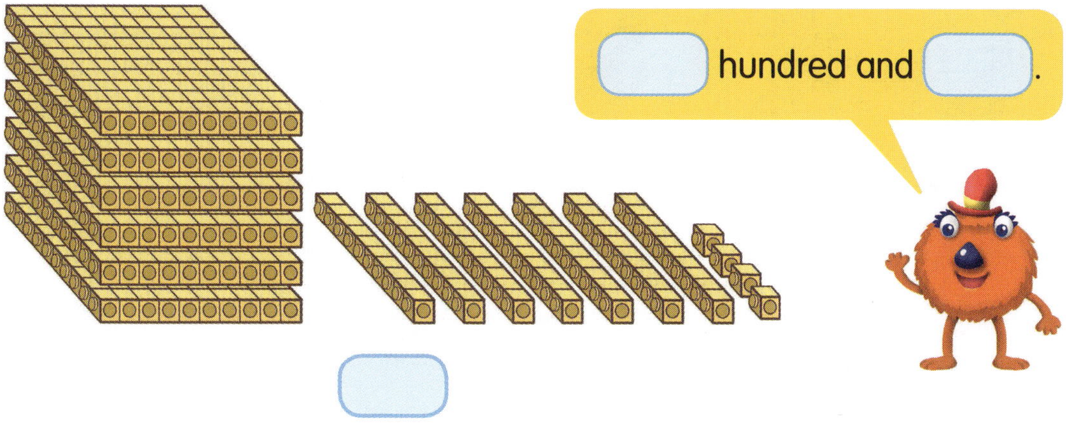

4 How many are there?

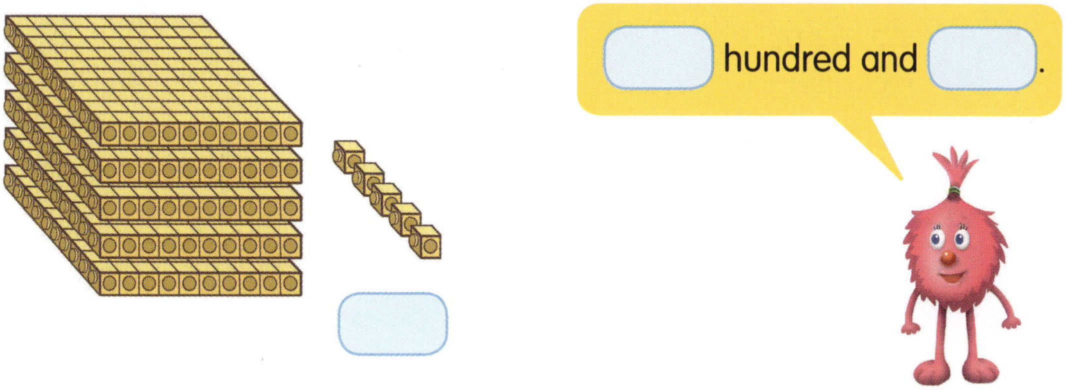

5

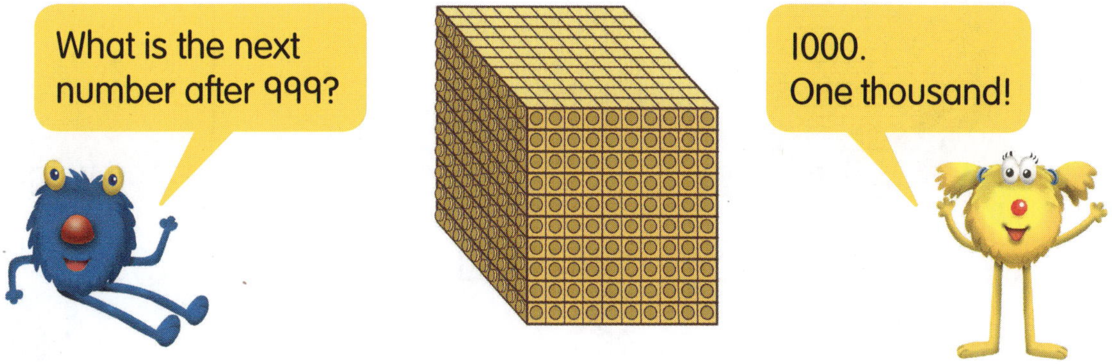

Counting on in ones

6

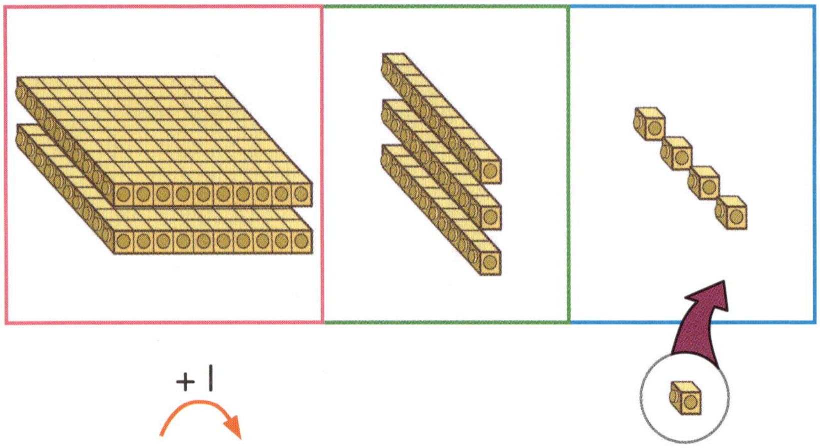

+ 1

234, 235

7 Count on in ones.

424, 425, 426, ___, ___, ___, ___, ___

Counting on in tens

8

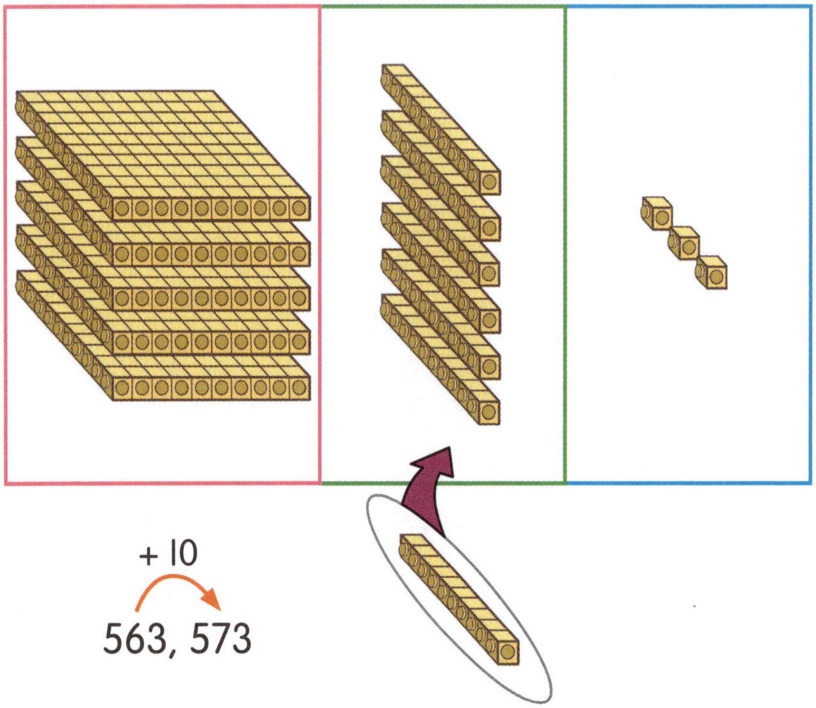

+ 10

563, 573

9 Count on in tens.

a 519, 529, 539, 549, ___, ___, ___, ___

b 740, 750, 760, 770, ___, ___, ___, ___

Counting on in hundreds

10

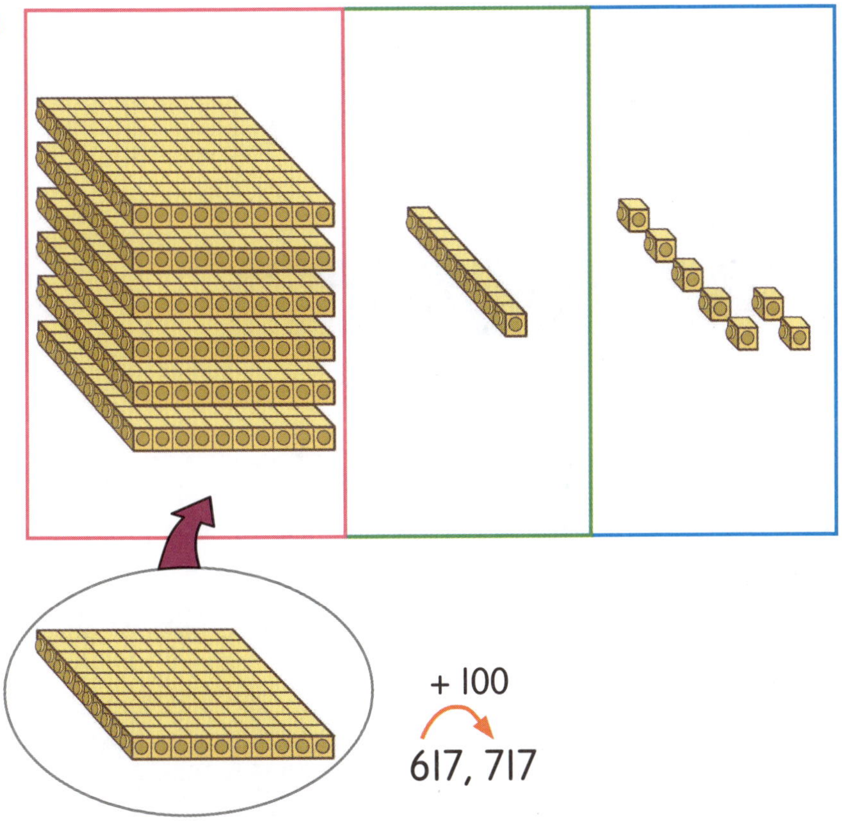

11 Count on in hundreds.

a 260, 360, 460, ___, ___, ___

b 435, 535, 635, ___, ___, ___

Practice Book 2A, p.5

Let's Learn!

Place value

1 How many cubes are there?

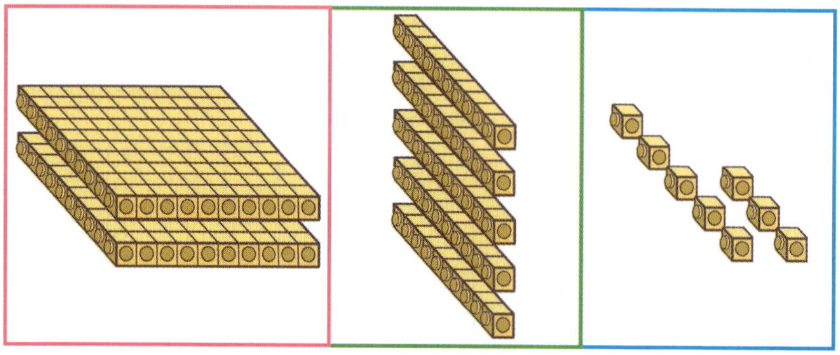

Hundreds	Tens	Ones
2	5	8
stands for 2 hundreds or 200	stands for 5 tens or 50	stands for 8 ones or 8

258 = 2 hundreds 5 tens 8 ones

258 = 200 + 50 + 8

In 258,

the digit 8 is in the ones place,
the digit 5 is in the tens place and
the digit 2 is in the hundreds place.

2

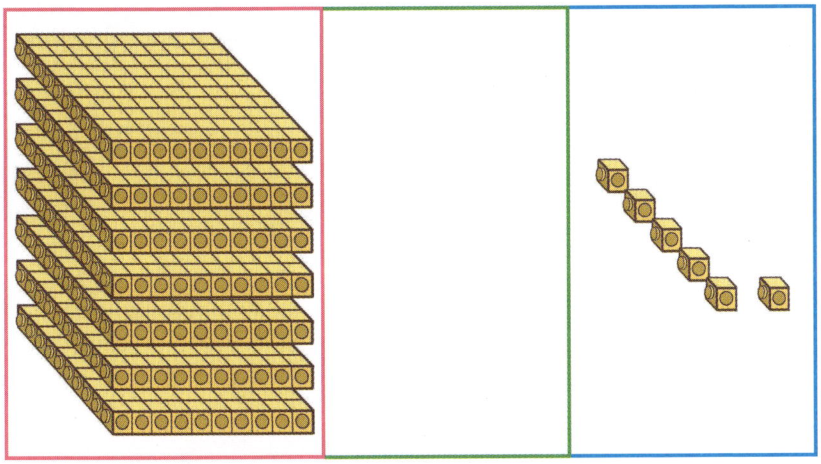

Hundreds	Tens	Ones
☐	☐	☐
stands for	stands for	stands for
☐ hundreds	☐ tens	☐ ones
or ☐	or ☐	or ☐

706 = ☐ hundreds ☐ tens ☐ ones

706 = ☐ + ☐ + ☐

In 706,

the digit ☐ is in the ones place,

the digit ☐ is in the tens place and

the digit ☐ is in the hundreds place.

3 Answer these questions.

a In 708,

the digit 7 is in the ______ place,

the digit 0 is in the ______ place and

the digit 8 is in the ______ place.

b In 960,

the digit in the hundreds place is ______,

the digit in the tens place is ______ and

the digit in the ones place is ______.

4

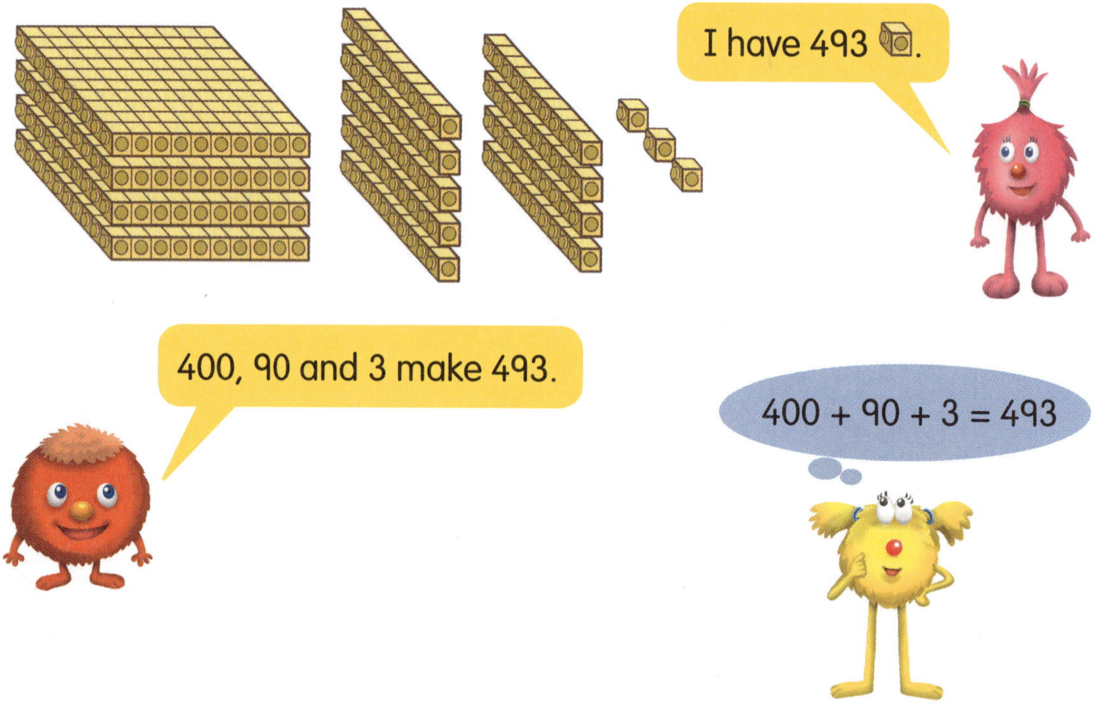

5 Find the missing numbers.

a 800, 60 and 7 make ______.

b 200 + 70 + 4 = ______

Game

Players: 2
You will need:
- base ten equipment
- place value charts

6 Show the number!

How to play:

1 Player 1 arranges some .

2 Player 2 counts the  and writes the number in the place value chart.

3 Player 1 checks the answer.

4 Take turns to show the  and write the numbers. Players get one point for each correct answer.

Play five rounds. The player with the most points wins!

Practice Book 2A, p.9

Let's Learn!

Comparing numbers within 1000

1 Which set contains the greater number?
Is it Set A or B?

Set A
235

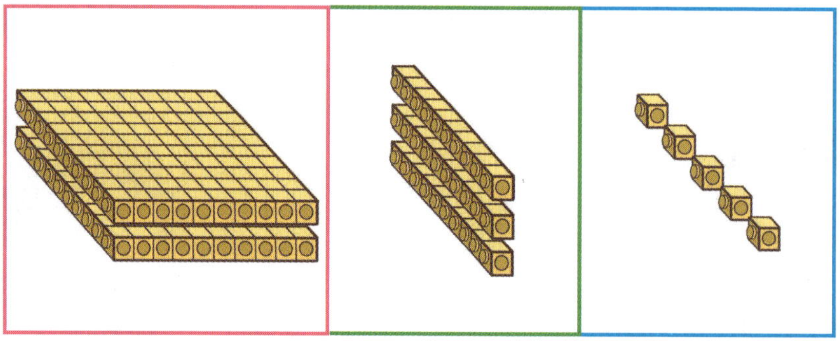

Set B
146

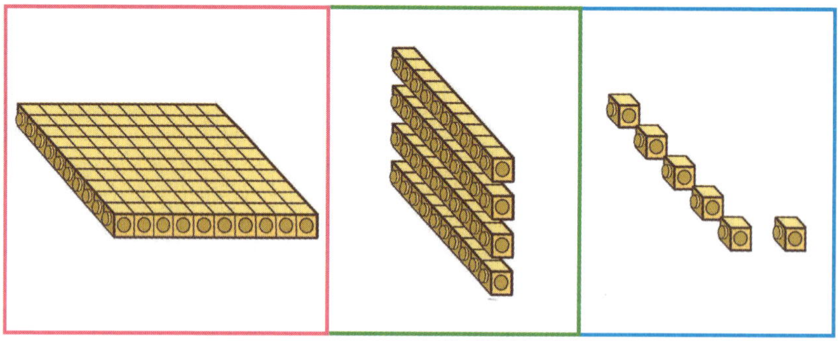

Compare the hundreds.

2 hundreds is greater than 1 hundred.

235 is greater than 146.
The number in Set A is greater than the number in Set B.

2

If two numbers have the same number of hundreds, we compare the tens.

Now choose the set that contains the smaller number.
Is it Set A or B?

Set A
372

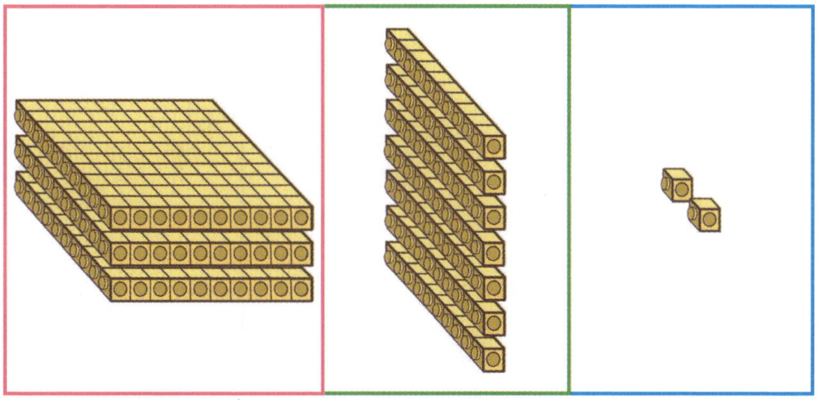

Set B
345

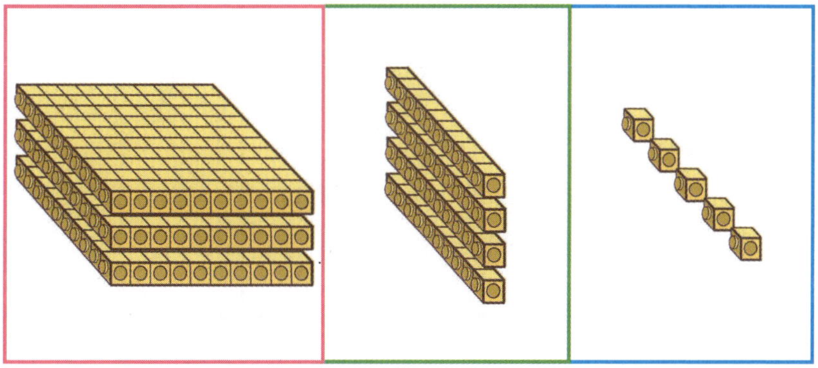

First compare the hundreds.
They are the same.
Then compare the tens.

4 tens is smaller than 7 tens.

345 is smaller than 372.
Set B is the smaller set.

3

If two numbers have the same number of hundreds and tens, we compare the ones.

Which is greater?
Which is smaller?

Set A
418

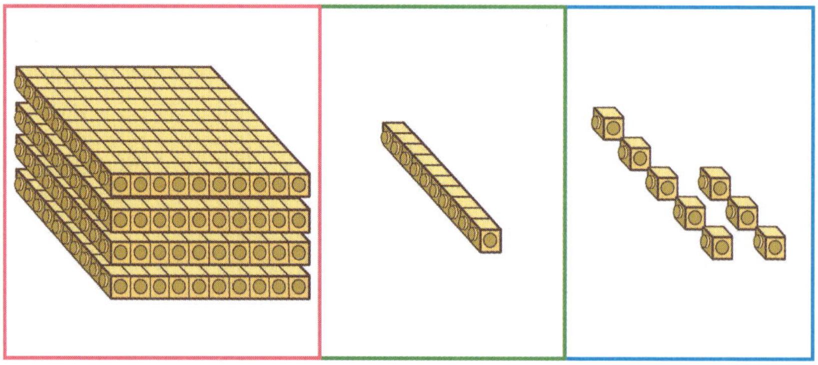

Set B
415

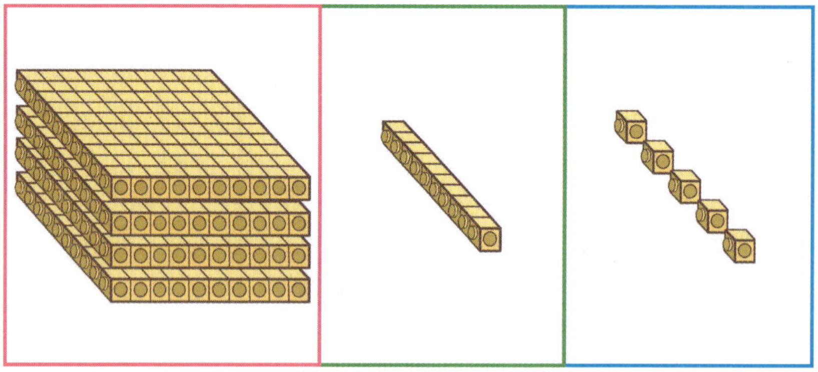

First compare the hundreds. Both are the same.

Then compare the tens. Both are the same.

Finally compare the ones. 5 ones is smaller than 8 ones.

418 is greater than 415.
415 is smaller than 418.

4 Which is greater?
Which is smaller?
Use **greater than** or **smaller than**.

a

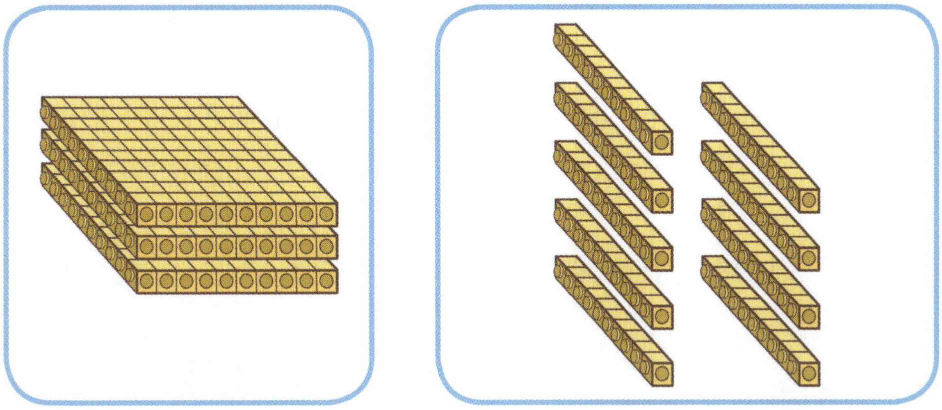

300 is ______ 90.

b

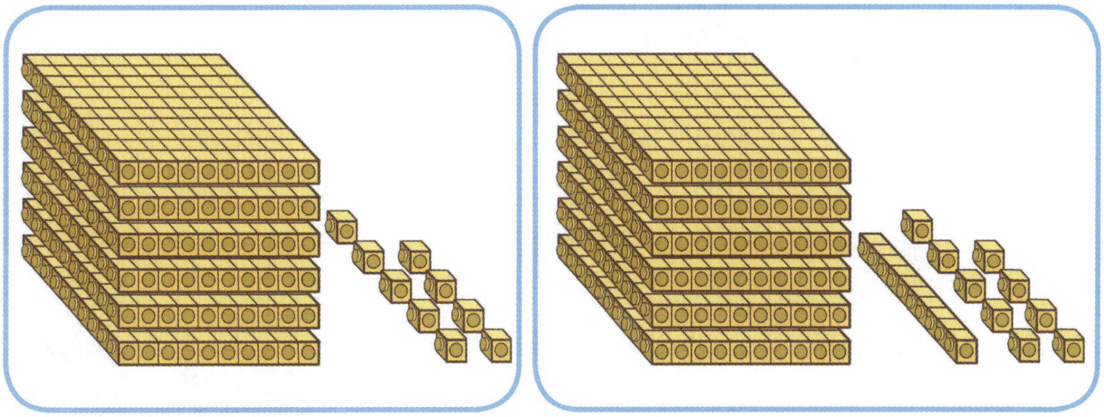

609 is ______ 619.

5 Use **greater than** or **smaller than** to write about these numbers.

a 233 is ______ 333.

b 715 is ______ 709.

c 564 is ______ 560.

d 479 is ______ 497.

Game

Players: 3

You will need:

- a 10-sided dice
- a piece of paper

6 Roll and Show!

How to play:

1 Player 1 rolls the dice three times to make a 3-digit number. Player 3 writes it down.

2 Player 2 rolls the dice three times to make another 3-digit number. Player 3 writes it down.

3 Player 3 looks at the numbers and writes **greater than** or **smaller than** between them. The other players check the answer.

4 Take turns to roll and write! Get one point for each correct answer.

Play five rounds. The player with the most points wins!

Practice Book 2A, p.15

Let's Learn!

Order and pattern

1 Put 489, 236 and 701 in order.
Begin with the smallest number.

	Hundreds	Tens	Ones
489	4	8	9
236	2	3	6
701	7	0	1

Compare the hundreds.

701 is greater than 489 and 236.

489 is greater than 236.

701 is the greatest.
236 is the smallest.

236, 489, 701

smallest

2 Put 459, 574 and 558 in order.
Begin with the greatest number.

	Hundreds	Tens	Ones
459	4	5	9
574	5	7	4
558	5	5	8

☐ is the greatest.

☐ is the smallest.

☐, ☐, ☐

greatest

Maths Journal

3 247 724 274 427

How do I compare the numbers so that I can order them from smallest to largest?

1 Which of these is correct?

a I compare the ones first, then the tens and finally the hundreds.

b I compare the tens first, then the hundreds and finally the ones.

c I compare the hundreds first, then the tens and finally the ones.

d I compare the hundreds first, then the ones and finally the tens.

2 Ella arranged the numbers in order, beginning with the smallest.

724 247 274 427

smallest

Was Ella correct?

Write a few sentences to explain if she was right or wrong.

Example

724 is not the smallest number because ...

4 Order these numbers. Begin with the smallest number.

a 707 904 762 555

b 368 555 357 699 553

5 The numbers on this number track follow a pattern.
There are missing numbers on the track.

1 more than 253 is 254.

243	244	245	246		248	249		251	252	253		255

1 more than 246 is 247.

1 less than 251 is 250.

The missing numbers are 247, 250 and 254.

6 The numbers on the track follow a pattern.
Find the missing numbers.

10 more than 821 is ☐.

721	731	741	751		771	781		801	811	821		841

10 more than 751 is ☐.

10 less than 801 is ☐.

7 The numbers on the steps follow a pattern.
Some numbers are missing.
Find the missing numbers.

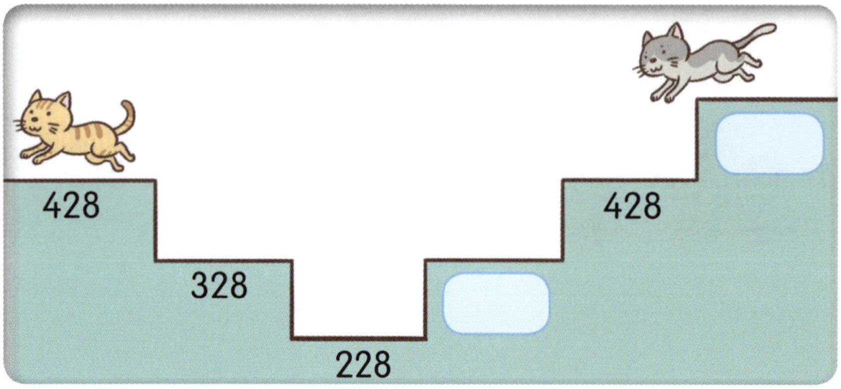

8 Answer these questions.

a 1 less than 999 is ______.

b 20 more than 415 is ______.

c 100 more than 900 is ______.

d 200 less than 635 is ______.

e 442, 542, 642, 742, ______, ______

f 884, 874, 864, ______, 844, ______

g 298, 299, ______, ______, 302, 303

h 342, ______, ______, ______, 338, 337

i ______, 810, 820, ______, ______, 850

j ______, ______, 332, 232, 132, ______

Home Maths Use the page numbers in a long book to introduce your child to numbers within 1000. Identify a page number and ask your child to locate a page number that is 1, 10 or 100 more or less than that page number.

Game

9 Roll and count!

How to play:

Players: 3 to 4

You will need:

- a 10-sided dice
- a piece of paper

1 Roll the dice three times to make a 3-digit number. If the 3-digit number is 900 or more, roll the dice three more times to make another 3-digit number.

2 Copy and complete this table.

Number made	
1 more than the number	
1 less than the number	
10 more than the number	
10 less than the number	
100 more than the number	
100 less than the number	

3 Take turns to roll and count! Get one point for each correct answer.

Play five rounds. The player with the most points wins!

Practice Book 2A, p.17

Let's Explore!

10 Ella and Peter want to know how many numbers there are from:

3 to 9   8 to 15   17 to 27

They find the answer in different ways.

I counted the numbers.
There are 7 numbers from 3 to 9.

I subtracted the numbers.
9 minus 3 is equal to 6.

Ella

Peter

	Ella's method	Peter's method
3 to 9	7	$9 - 3 = 6$
8 to 15	8	$15 - 8 = 7$
17 to 27	11	$27 - 17 = 10$

Millie

Millie checks the answers and shows that Ella's method is correct.
Then she looks at Peter's and Ella's answers and sees a pattern.
Ella's answer is always 1 more than Peter's answer.

Let's Explore!

Subtract the numbers and add 1 to find how many numbers there are from:

a 22 to 38 **b** 44 to 79 **c** 24 to 94

Check your answers by counting.

Put On Your Thinking Caps!

11 **a** Find the missing numbers.

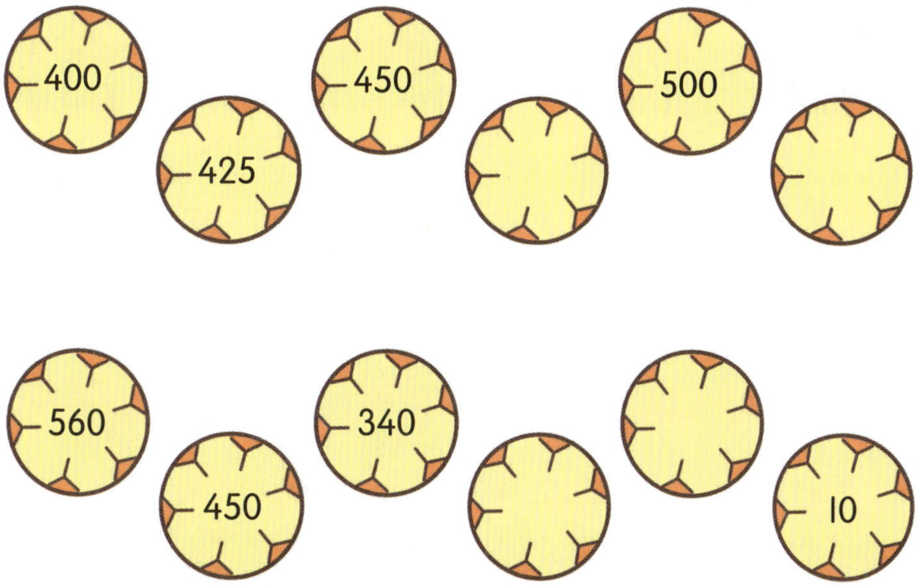

Put On Your Thinking Caps!

b A squirrel has been storing food for the winter and has already stored some nuts.
The squirrel adds 3 more nuts to its food store every day.
The squirrel does this for 5 days.
At the end of the fifth day, the squirrel has stored 50 nuts.

How many nuts did the squirrel have at the end of the first day?

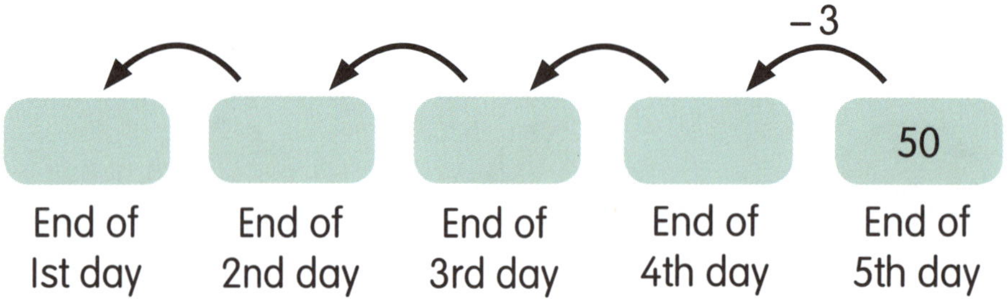

If the squirrel continues to add 3 nuts to the food store every day, how many more days does the squirrel need to store 62 nuts?

Practice Book 2A, p.19
Practice Book 2A, p.21

Unit 2 Addition and Subtraction within 1000

Let's Learn!

Simple addition within 1000

1 Add using base ten equipment.
Use the place value chart to help you.

a 123 + 5 = ?

123

5

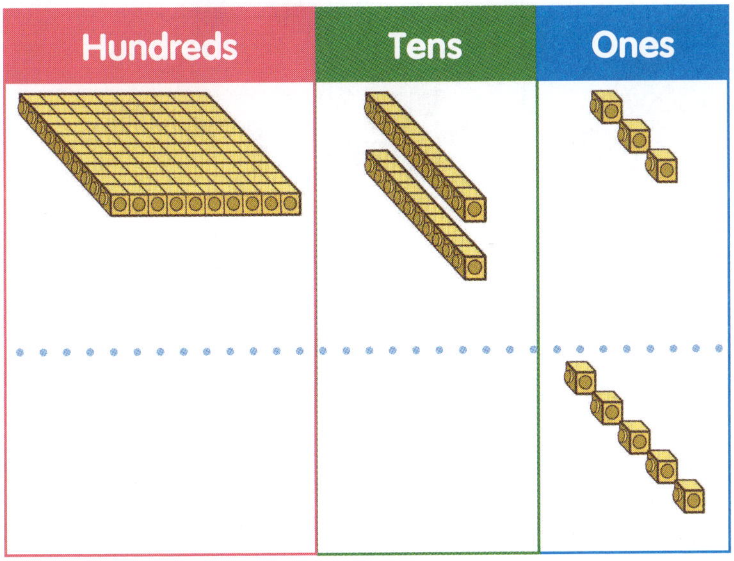

123 + 5 = 128

First add the ones.

$$\begin{array}{r} 1\ 2\ 3 \\ +\quad\ \ 5 \\ \hline 8 \\ \hline \end{array}$$

3 ones + 5 ones
= 8 ones

Then add the tens.

$$\begin{array}{r} 1\ 2\ 3 \\ +\quad\ \ 5 \\ \hline 2\ 8 \\ \hline \end{array}$$

2 tens + 0 tens
= 2 tens

Finally add
the hundreds.

$$\begin{array}{r} 1\ 2\ 3 \\ +\quad\ \ 5 \\ \hline 1\ 2\ 8 \\ \hline \end{array}$$

1 hundred + 0 hundreds
= 1 hundred

b 271 + 27 = ?

271

27

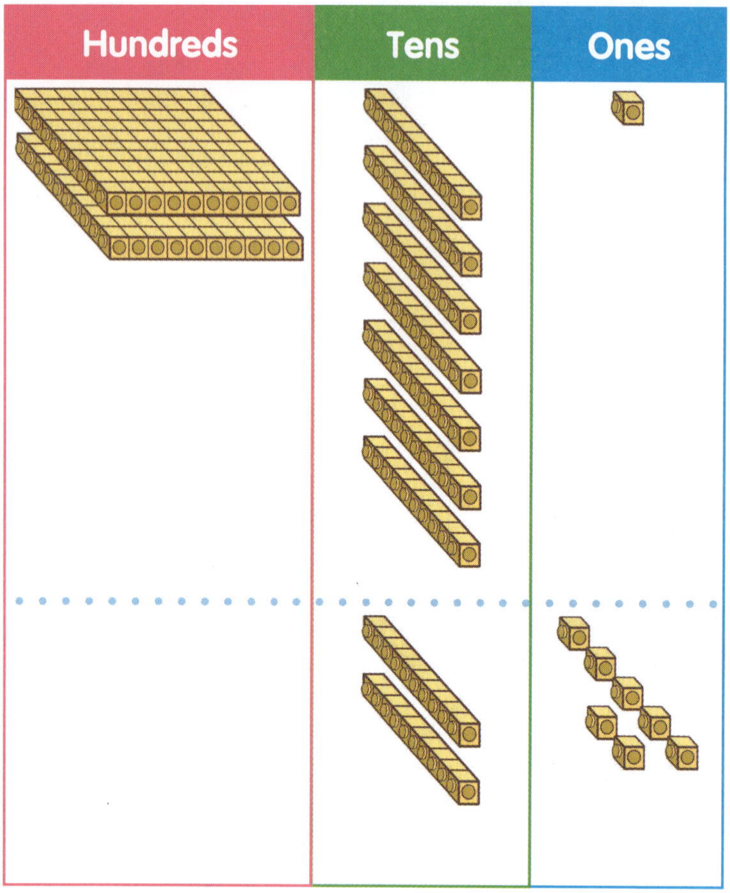

First add the ones.

$$\begin{array}{r} 2\,7\,1 \\ +\;\;\;2\,7 \\ \hline 8 \\ \hline \end{array}$$

1 one + 7 ones
= 8 ones

Then add the tens.

$$\begin{array}{r} 2\,7\,1 \\ +\;\;\;2\,7 \\ \hline 9\,8 \\ \hline \end{array}$$

7 tens + 2 tens
= 9 tens

Finally add
the hundreds.

$$\begin{array}{r} 2\,7\,1 \\ +\;\;\;2\,7 \\ \hline 2\,9\,8 \\ \hline \end{array}$$

2 hundreds + 0 hundreds
= 2 hundreds

271 + 27 = 298

2 Complete these.

a 153 + 4

b 181 + 6

c 371 + 24

d 706 + 83

3 135 + 342 = ?

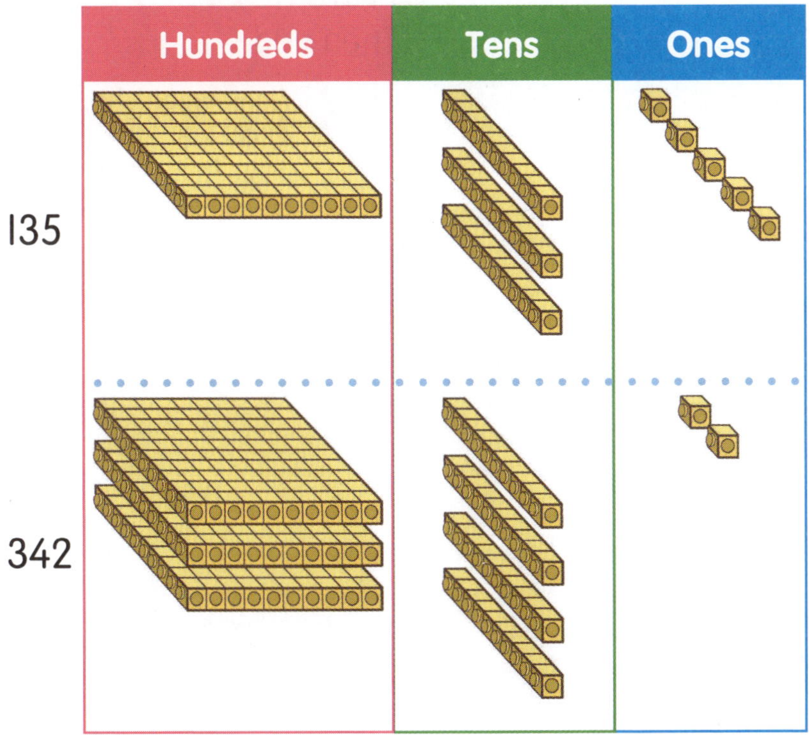

First add the ones.

$$\begin{array}{r} 1\,3\,5 \\ +\ 3\,4\,2 \\ \hline 7 \end{array}$$

5 ones + 2 ones
= 7 ones

Then add the tens.

$$\begin{array}{r} 1\,3\,5 \\ +\ 3\,4\,2 \\ \hline 7\,7 \end{array}$$

3 tens + 4 tens
= 7 tens

Finally add
the hundreds.

$$\begin{array}{r} 1\,3\,5 \\ +\ 3\,4\,2 \\ \hline 4\,7\,7 \end{array}$$

1 hundred + 3 hundreds
= 4 hundreds

135 + 342 = 477

4 623 + 254 = ?

First add the ones.
3 ones + 4 ones = ☐ ones

Then add the tens.
2 tens + 5 tens = ☐ tens

Finally add the hundreds.
6 hundreds + 2 hundreds = ☐ hundreds

623 + 254 = ☐

Write 623 + 254 in this way.
Then add.

```
  6 2 3
+ 2 5 4
-------
    ☐
-------
```

5 Solve these word problems.

a Peter sells 445 raffle tickets.
Miya sells 321 raffle tickets.
How many raffle tickets do they sell altogether?

b 216 children go to a farm on Saturday.
102 more children go to the farm on Sunday than on Saturday.
How many children go to the farm on Sunday?

Practice Book 2A, pp.23 and 25

Let's Learn!

Simple subtraction within 1000

1 Subtract using base ten equipment.
Use the place value chart to help you.

a 384 – 3 = ?

384

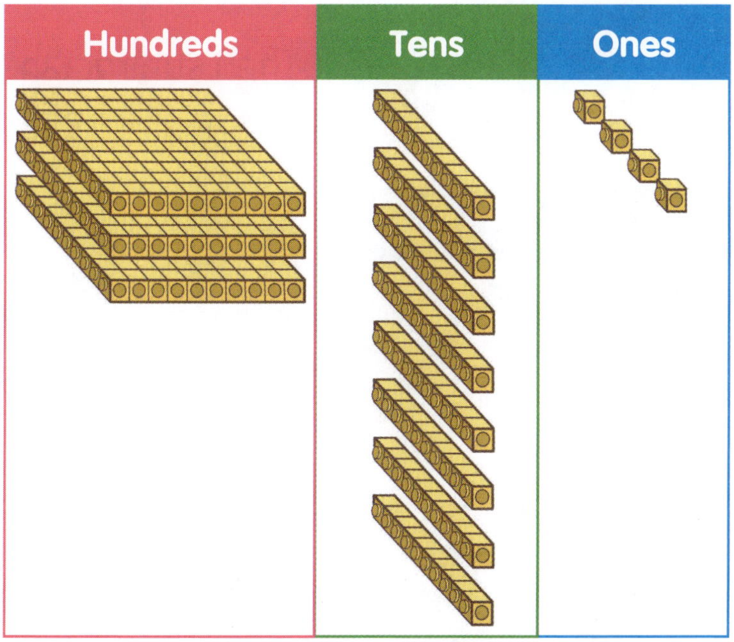

381

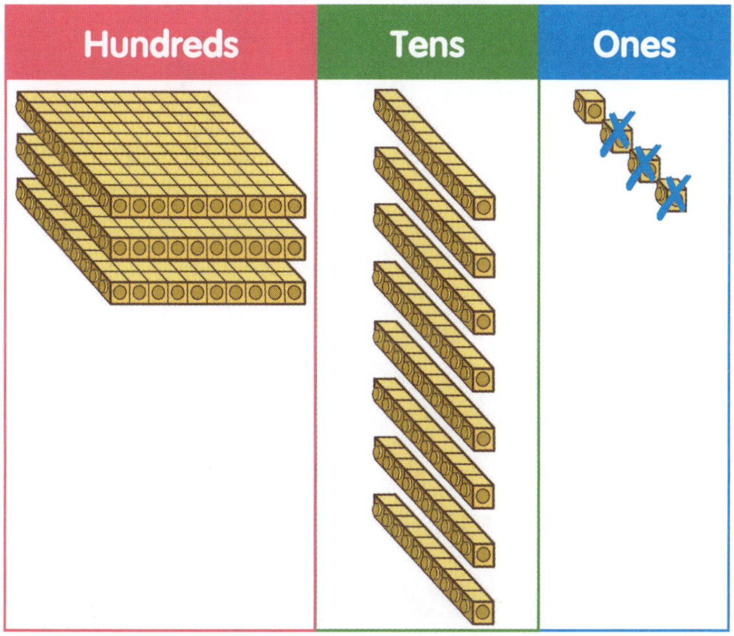

First subtract the ones.

```
  3 8 4
–     3
-------
      1
```

4 ones – 3 ones
= 1 one

Then subtract the tens.

```
  3 8 4
–     3
-------
    8 1
```

8 tens – 0 tens
= 8 tens

Finally subtract the hundreds.

```
  3 8 4
–     3
-------
  3 8 1
```

3 hundreds – 0 hundreds
= 3 hundreds

384 – 3 = 381

b 459 – 46 = ?

459

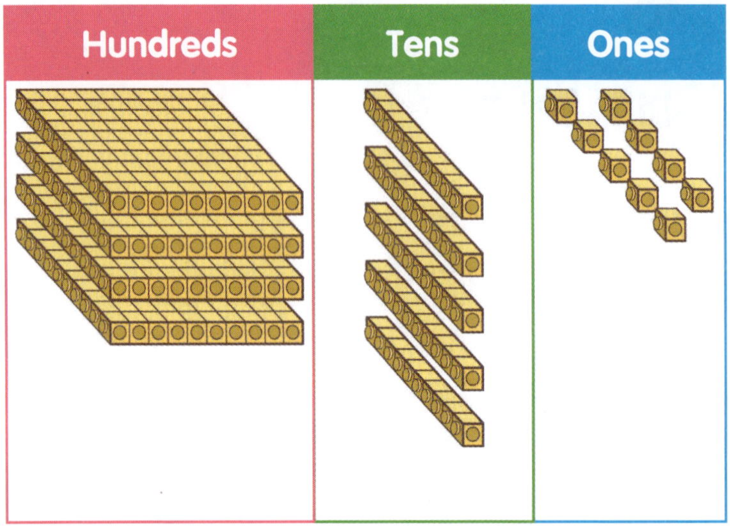

First subtract the ones.

$$\begin{array}{r} 459 \\ -\ \ 46 \\ \hline 3 \end{array}$$

9 ones – 6 ones
= 3 ones

Then subtract the tens.

$$\begin{array}{r} 459 \\ -\ \ 46 \\ \hline 13 \end{array}$$

5 tens – 4 tens
= 1 ten

413

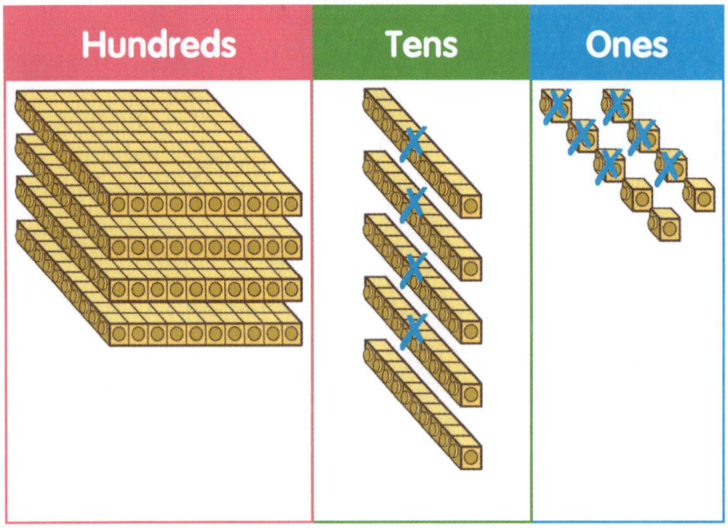

Finally subtract the hundreds.

$$\begin{array}{r} 459 \\ -\ \ 46 \\ \hline 413 \end{array}$$

4 hundreds – 0 hundreds
= 4 hundreds

459 – 46 = 413

2 Complete these.

a 408 – 6

b 299 – 8

c 655 – 40

d 348 – 27

3 249 – 134 = ?

249

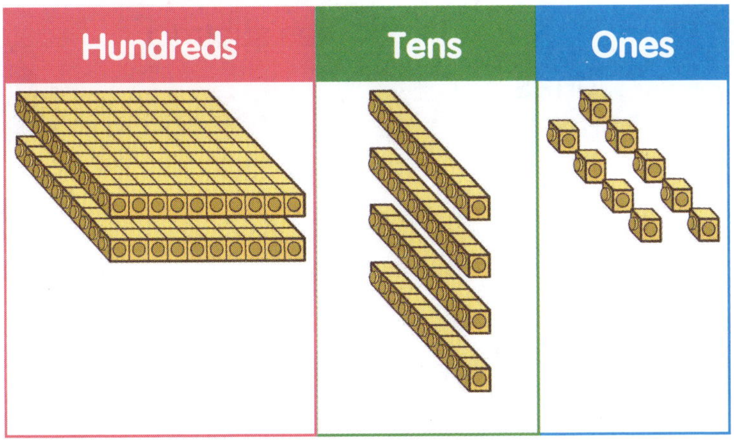

First subtract the ones.

$$\begin{array}{r} 2\,4\,9 \\ -\ 1\,3\,4 \\ \hline 5 \end{array}$$

9 ones – 4 ones
= 5 ones

115

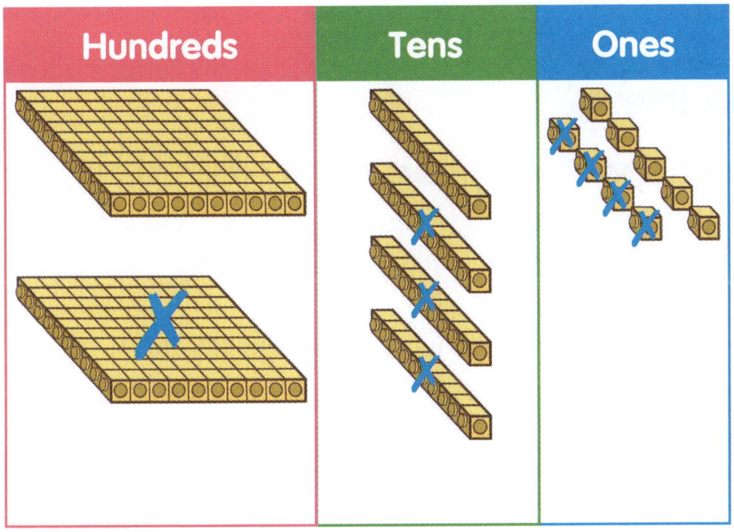

Then subtract the tens.

$$\begin{array}{r} 2\,4\,9 \\ -\ 1\,3\,4 \\ \hline 1\,5 \end{array}$$

4 tens – 3 tens
= 1 ten

Finally subtract the hundreds.

$$\begin{array}{r} 2\,4\,9 \\ -\ 1\,3\,4 \\ \hline 1\,1\,5 \end{array}$$

2 hundreds – 1 hundred
= 1 hundred

249 – 134 = 115

4 327 – 115 = ?

$$\begin{array}{r} 3\ 2\ 7 \\ -\ 1\ 1\ 5 \\ \hline \square \\ \hline \end{array}$$

First subtract the ones.
7 ones – 5 ones = ☐ ones

Then subtract the tens.
2 tens – 1 ten = ☐ ten

Finally subtract the hundreds.
3 hundreds – 1 hundred = ☐ hundreds

327 – 115 = ☐

5 Solve these word problems.

a Farha picks 363 apples and pears at an orchard.
She picks 23 pears.
How many apples does Farha pick?

b There are 999 children watching a football match.
447 of them are boys.
How many girls are there?

Practice Book 2A, pp.27 and 29

Let's Learn!

Addition with regrouping the ones

1 347 + 129 = ?

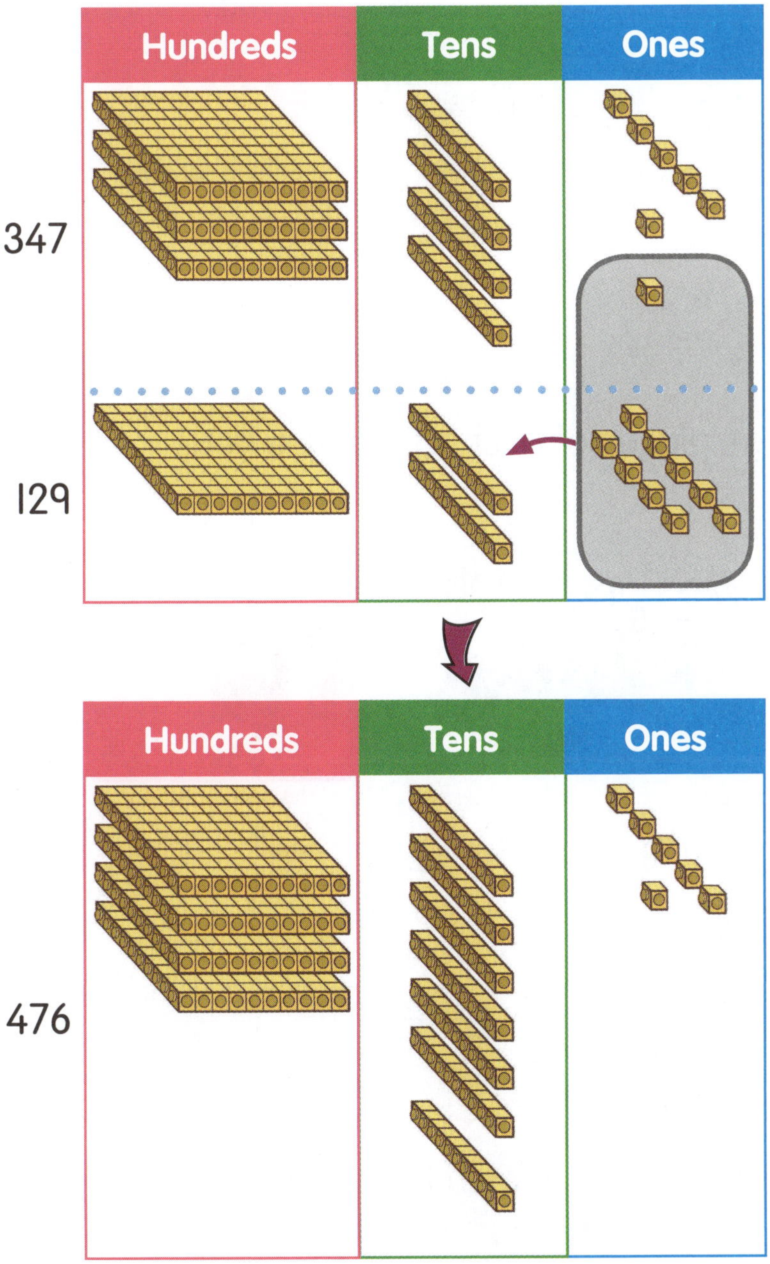

347 + 129 = 476

First add the ones.

$$\begin{array}{r} 3\,4\,7 \\ +\;1\,2\,9 \\ \hline 6 \\ \hline {\scriptstyle 1}\;\; \end{array}$$

7 ones + 9 ones
= 16 ones

Regroup the ones.
16 ones = 1 ten 6 ones

Then add the tens.

$$\begin{array}{r} 3\,4\,7 \\ +\;1\,2\,9 \\ \hline 7\,6 \\ \hline {\scriptstyle 1}\;\;\; \end{array}$$

4 tens + 2 tens + 1 ten
= 7 tens

Finally add
the hundreds.

$$\begin{array}{r} 3\,4\,7 \\ +\;1\,2\,9 \\ \hline 4\,7\,6 \\ \hline {\scriptstyle 1}\;\;\; \end{array}$$

3 hundreds + 1 hundred
= 4 hundreds

2 136 + 127 = ?

First add the ones.
6 ones + 7 ones = ☐ ones

Regroup the ones.

☐ ones = 1 ten ☐ ones

Then add the tens.
3 tens + 2 tens + 1 ten = ☐ tens

Finally add the hundreds.
1 hundred + 1 hundred = ☐ hundreds

136 + 127 = ☐

```
  1 3 6
+ 1 2 7
-------
   ☐
-------
```

3 Add the numbers. Use place value charts to help you.

Example

```
  6 4 5
+ 2 3 5
-------
  8 8 0
-------
    1
```

a
```
  4 2 4
+ 4 3 9
-------
   ☐
-------
```

b
```
  3 1 8
+ 5 2 8
-------
   ☐
-------
```

c
```
  7 0 6
+ 2 7 4
-------
   ☐
-------
```

d
```
  4 0 5
+ 5 8 8
-------
   ☐
-------
```

4 Solve these word problems.

a 637 children and 257 adults watch a parade.
How many people watch the parade altogether?

b At the fair Peter sells 162 scoops of vanilla ice cream and 119 scoops of chocolate ice cream.
How many scoops of ice cream does Peter sell altogether?

Game

Players: 3 to 4

You will need:
- two dice
- base ten equipment

5 Make a square!

How to play:

I Roll two dice. Add the numbers you get.

2 Take this number of . You can swap I0 , for I . Take turns to play.

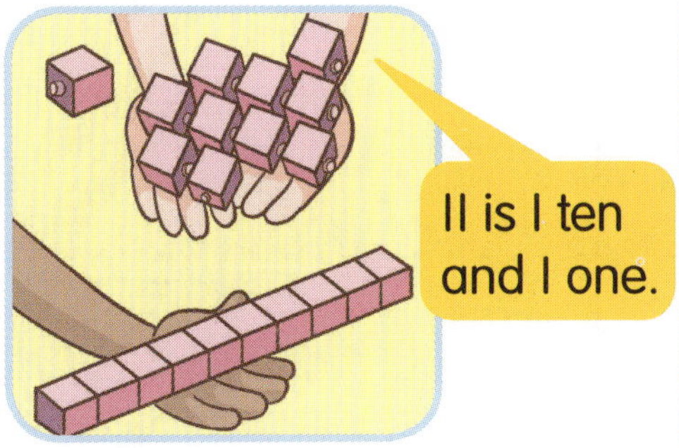

3 When it is your turn again, roll the dice. Take this number of . Add to the and you have.

The first player to get I0 to make I wins!

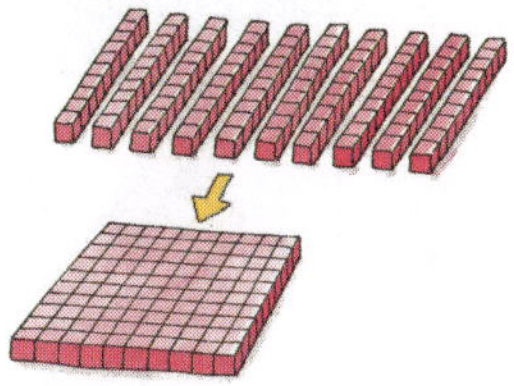

Practice Book 2A, pp.3I and 33

Let's Learn!

Addition with regrouping the tens

1 182 + 93 = ?

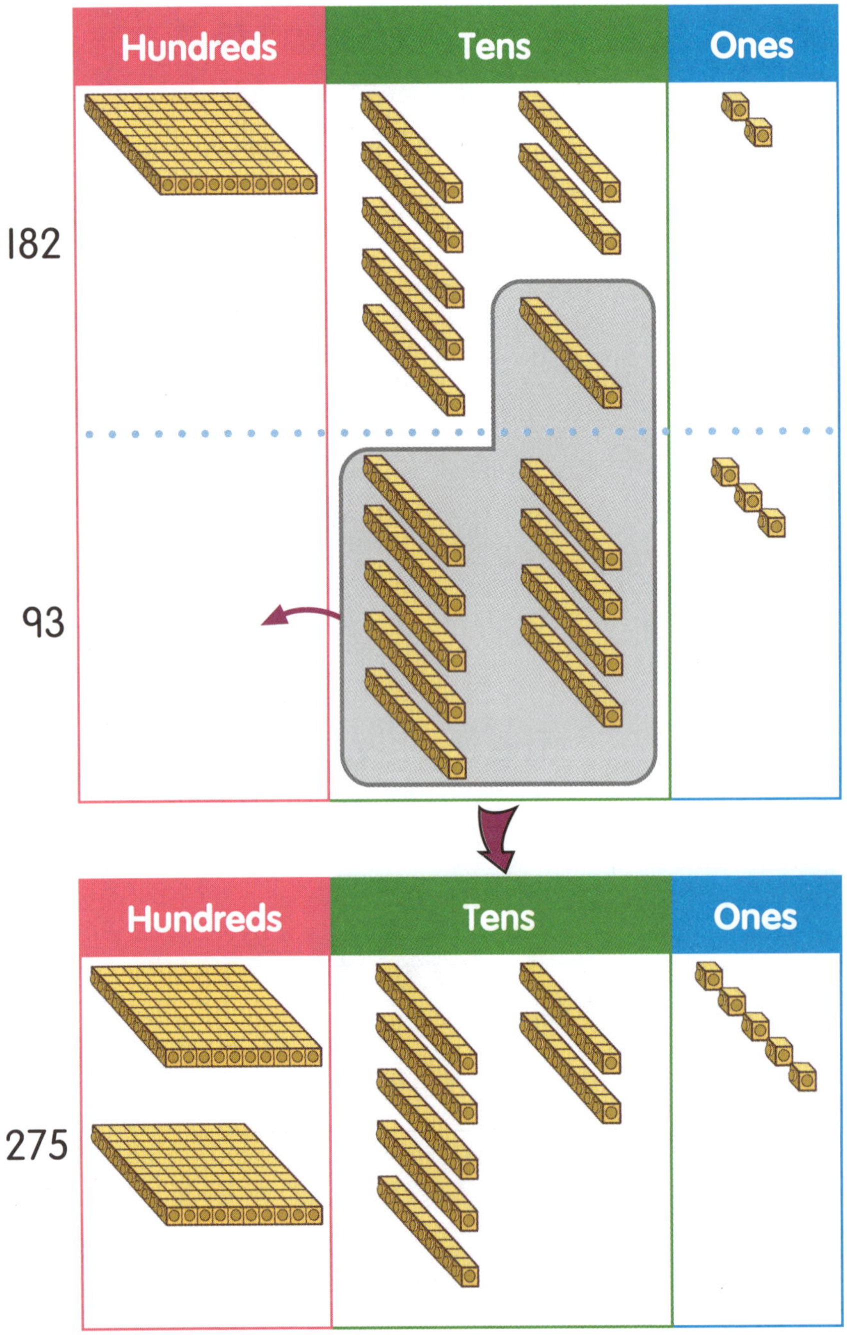

First add the ones.

$$\begin{array}{r} 1\,8\,2 \\ +\quad 9\,3 \\ \hline 5 \\ \hline \end{array}$$

2 ones + 3 ones
= 5 ones

Then add the tens.

$$\begin{array}{r} 1\,8\,2 \\ +\quad 9\,3 \\ \hline 7\,5 \\ \hline {\scriptstyle 1}\quad\;\; \end{array}$$

8 tens + 9 tens
= 17 tens

Regroup the tens.
17 tens
= 1 hundred 7 tens

Finally add
the hundreds.

$$\begin{array}{r} 1\,8\,2 \\ +\quad 9\,3 \\ \hline 2\,7\,5 \\ \hline {\scriptstyle 1}\quad\;\; \end{array}$$

1 hundred + 1 hundred
= 2 hundreds

182 + 93 = 275

2 361 + 170 = ?

First add the ones.
1 one + 0 ones = ____ one

Then add the tens.
6 tens + 7 tens = ____ tens

Regroup the tens.

____ tens = 1 hundred ____ tens

Finally add the hundreds.
3 hundreds + 1 hundred + 1 hundred = ____ hundreds

361 + 170 = ____

Write 361 + 170 in this way.
Then add.

```
   3 6 1
 + 1 7 0
 -------
   ____
 -------
```

3 Use place value charts to help you add.

Example

```
   1 4 3
 +   8 1
 -------
   2 2 4
 -------
   1
```

4 tens + 8 tens = 12 tens
12 tens = 1 hundred 2 tens

a

```
   4 9 0
 + 1 3 5
 -------
   ____
 -------
```

b

```
   3 8 4
 + 5 5 2
 -------
   ____
 -------
```

c

```
   5 3 5
 + 1 7 4
 -------
   ____
 -------
```

d 266 + 562 **e** 730 + 98 **f** 345 + 264

4 543 cars and 274 buses pass Ella's school.
How many cars and buses pass Ella's school altogether?

Practice Book 2A, pp.35 and 37

Let's Learn!

Addition with regrouping the tens and ones

1 278 + 386 = ?

278

386

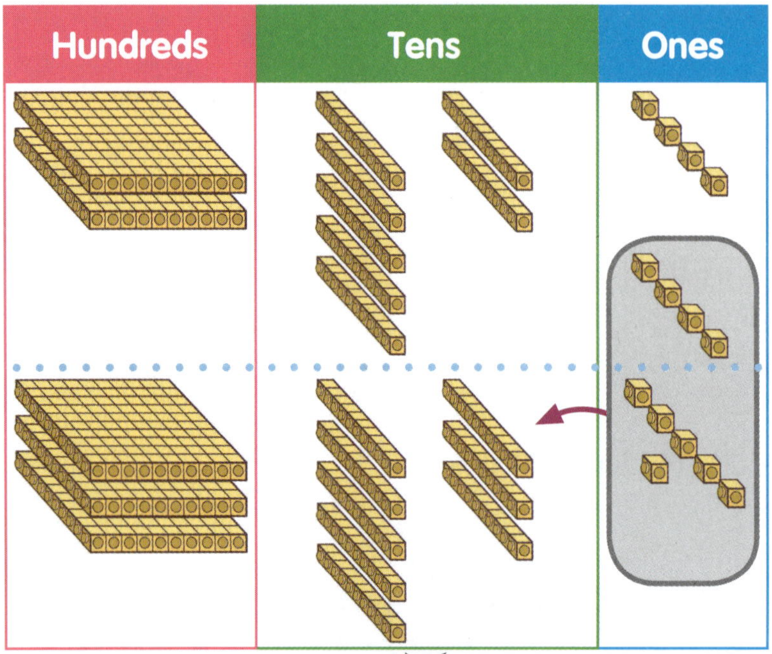

First add the ones.

$$\begin{array}{r} 2\,7\,8 \\ +\;3\,8\,6 \\ \hline 4 \\ \hline {\scriptstyle 1}\;\; \end{array}$$

8 ones + 6 ones
= 14 ones

Regroup the ones.
14 ones = 1 ten 4 ones

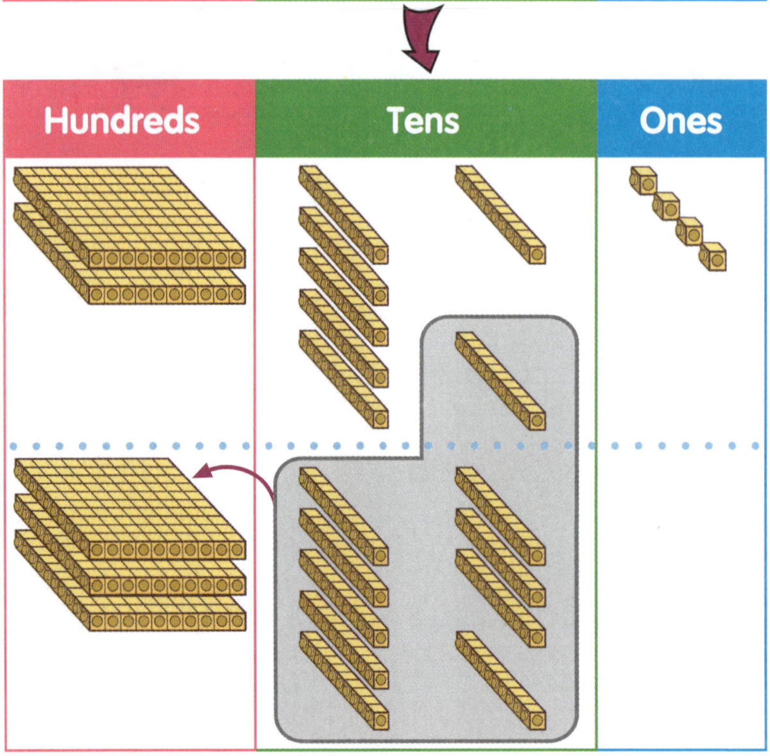

Then add the tens.

$$\begin{array}{r} 2\,7\,8 \\ +\;3\,8\,6 \\ \hline 6\,4 \\ \hline {\scriptstyle 1}\;{\scriptstyle 1}\;\; \end{array}$$

7 tens + 8 tens + 1 ten
= 16 tens

Regroup the tens.
16 tens
= 1 hundred 6 tens

664

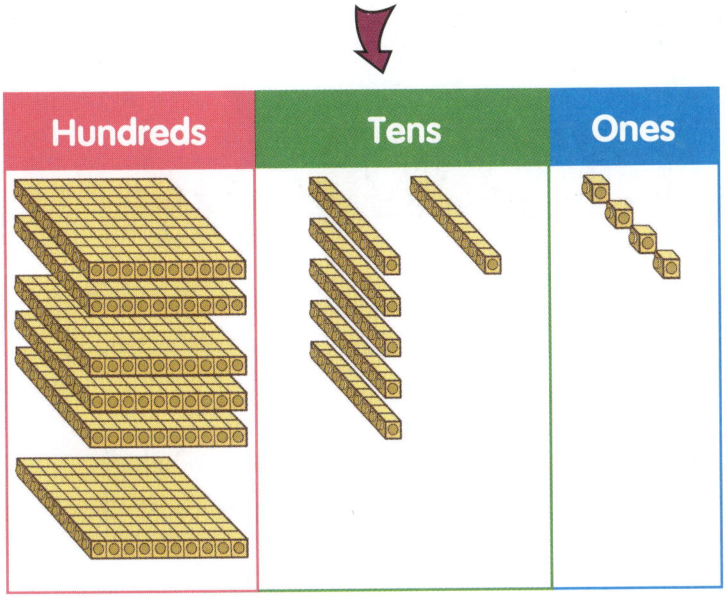

Finally add the hundreds.

```
  2 7 8
+ 3 8 6
-------
  6 6 4
  1 1
```

2 hundreds + 3 hundreds + 1 hundred = 6 hundreds

278 + 386 = 664

2 153 + 449 = ?

First add the ones.

3 ones + 9 ones = ☐ ones

Regroup the ones.

☐ ones = 1 ten ☐ ones

Then add the tens.

5 tens + 4 tens + 1 ten = ☐ tens

Regroup the tens.

☐ tens = 1 hundred ☐ tens

Finally add the hundreds.

1 hundred + 4 hundreds + 1 hundred = ☐ hundreds

153 + 449 = ☐

Write 153 + 449 in this way. Then add.

```
  1 5 3
+ 4 4 9
-------
   ☐
-------
```

3 Use place value charts to help you add.

Example

```
  5 0 9
+ 2 9 3
-------
  8 0 2
-------
  1 1
```

Remember to change 10 ones to 1 ten and 10 tens to 1 hundred!

a
```
  7 6 8
+ 1 5 6
-------
[    ]
-------
```

b
```
  3 7 2
+ 3 7 9
-------
[    ]
-------
```

c
```
  3 1 8
+ 4 8 5
-------
[    ]
-------
```

d 68 + 132

e 459 + 273

f 74 + 436

4 Solve these word problems.

a Millie sold 436 apples this morning.
She sold another 276 apples in the afternoon.
How many apples did Millie sell altogether?

b Mr Lee has 784 toy cars in a box.
He puts another 96 toy cars into the box.
How many toy cars does Mr Lee have altogether?

c Jack sold 468 balloons yesterday.
He sold 262 more balloons today than yesterday.
How many balloons did Jack sell today?

Practice Book 2A, pp.39 and 41

Let's Explore!

Players: 2 to 4

You will need:

- three sets of number cards from 0 to 9
- pencil and paper

5 Go for the greatest!

How to play:

1 You need three cards for each number.

2 Shuffle the cards. Give each player six cards.

3 Use the six cards to make as many 3-digit numbers as possible. Write them down.

4 Add any two 3-digit numbers. If the hundreds digits add up to 9 or more, choose another two numbers from your list.

The player with the greatest answer wins!

Let's Learn!

Subtraction with regrouping the tens and ones

1 242 – 128 = ?

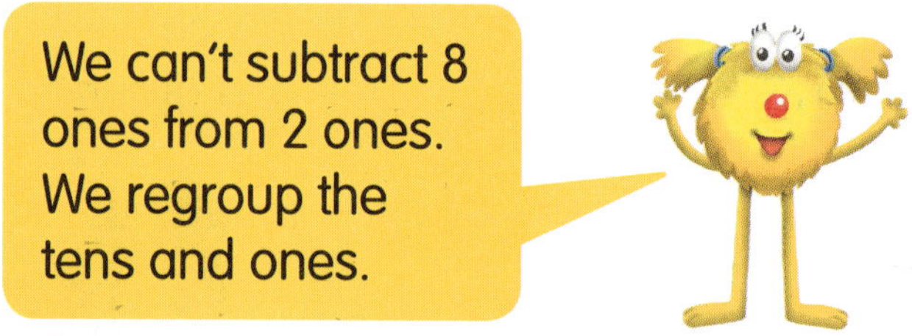

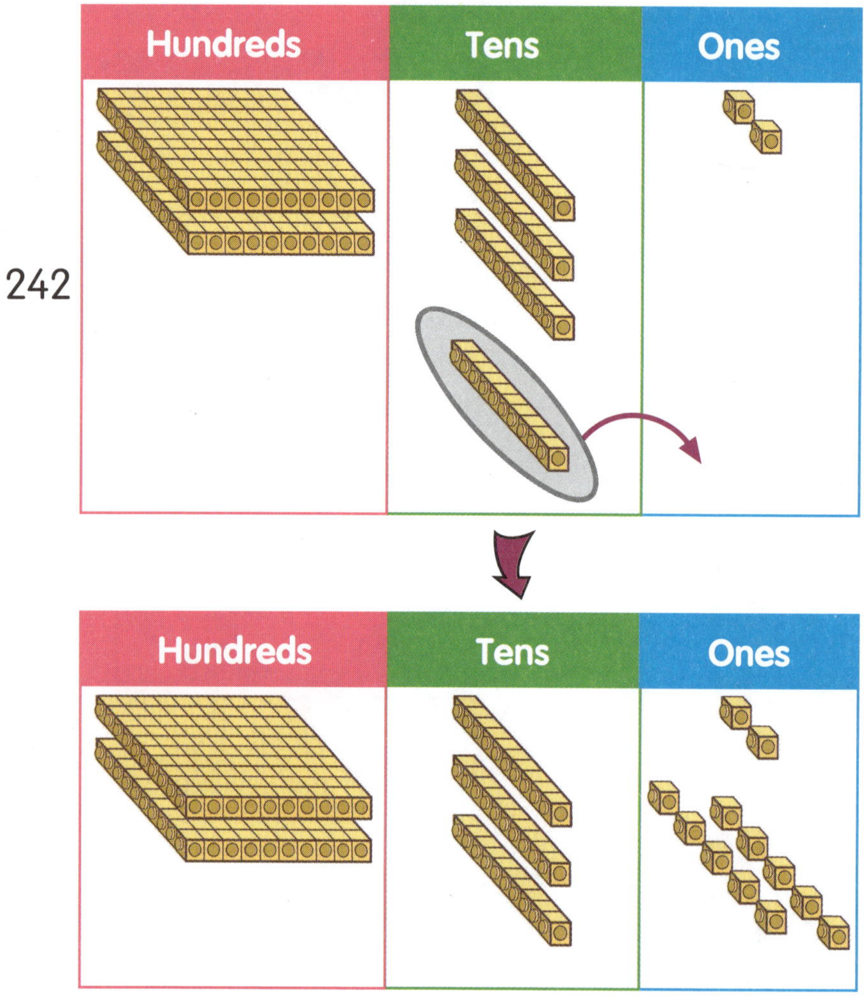

Regroup the tens and ones.

$$\begin{array}{r} 2\ {}^{3}\not{4}\ {}^{1}2 \\ -\ 1\ 2\ 8 \\ \hline 4 \\ \hline \end{array}$$

4 tens 2 ones
= 3 tens 12 ones

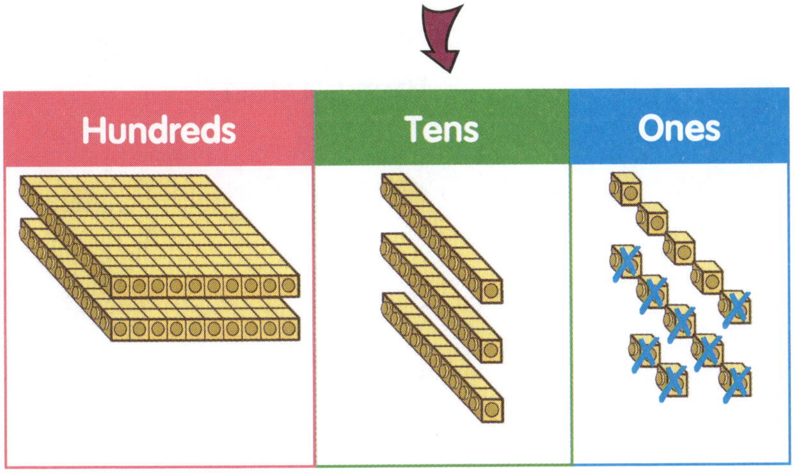

First subtract the ones.

$$\begin{array}{rrrr} & 2 & {}^{3}\cancel{4} & {}^{1}2 \\ - & 1 & 2 & 8 \\ \hline & & & 4 \end{array}$$

12 ones – 8 ones
= 4 ones

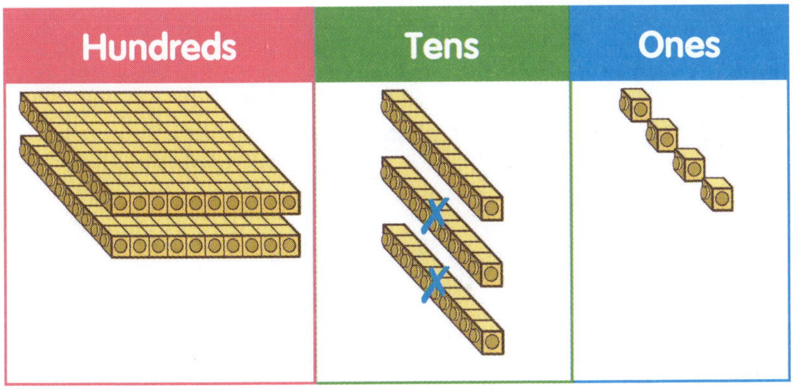

Then subtract the tens.

$$\begin{array}{rrrr} & 2 & {}^{3}\cancel{4} & {}^{1}2 \\ - & 1 & 2 & 8 \\ \hline & & 1 & 4 \end{array}$$

3 tens – 2 tens = 1 ten

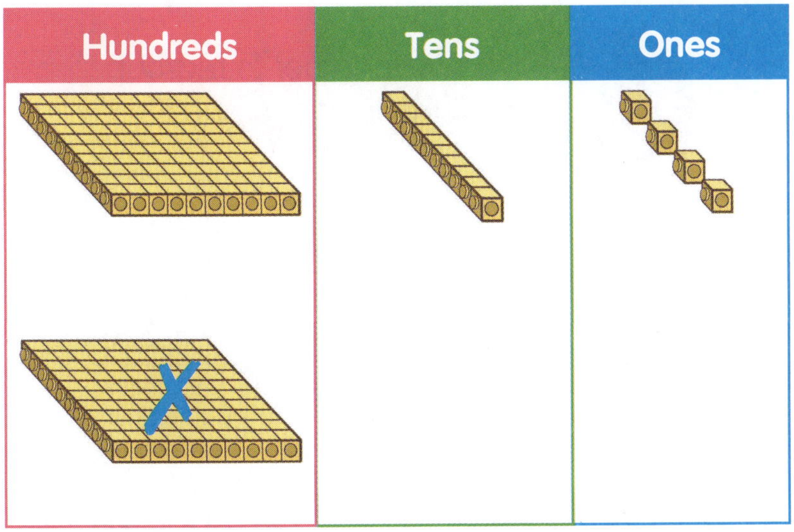

114

Finally subtract the hundreds.

$$\begin{array}{rrrr} & 2 & {}^{3}\cancel{4} & {}^{1}2 \\ - & 1 & 2 & 8 \\ \hline & 1 & 1 & 4 \end{array}$$

2 hundreds – 1 hundred
= 1 hundred

242 – 128 = 114

2 763 – 207 = ?

Regroup the tens and ones.

63 = 6 tens ☐ ones

= 5 tens ☐ ones

First subtract the ones.

☐ ones – ☐ ones = ☐ ones

Then subtract the tens.

5 tens – 0 tens = ☐ tens

Finally subtract the hundreds.

7 hundreds – 2 hundreds = ☐ hundreds

763 – 207 = ☐

Write 763 – 207 in this way.
Then subtract.

```
  7 6 3
– 2 0 7
-------
   ☐
-------
```

3 Subtract the numbers.
Use place value charts to help you subtract.

Example

```
  2 ⁸9̸ ¹1
–    5 5
--------
  2 3 6
--------
```

Remember to regroup the tens and ones!

a
```
  5 4 8
– 3 1 9
-------
   ☐
-------
```

b
```
  9 7 7
– 4 5 9
-------
   ☐
-------
```

c
```
  8 8 0
– 6 5 6
-------
   ☐
-------
```

d 992 – 879 **e** 783 – 69 **f** 416 – 307

4 A car park has 781 spaces.
472 spaces are taken. The rest are empty.
How many spaces are empty?

Practice Book 2A, pp.43 and 45

Let's Learn!

Subtraction with regrouping the hundreds and tens

1 537 – 272 = ?

537

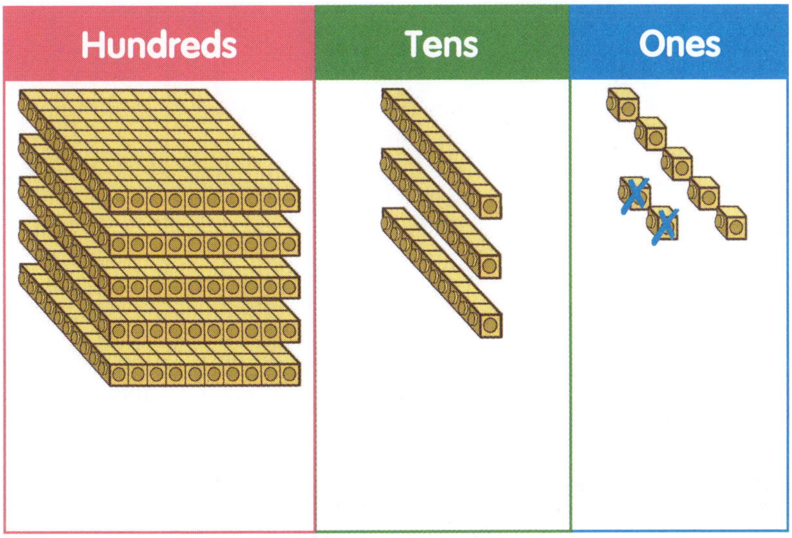

First subtract the ones.

```
  5 3 7
– 2 7 2
-------
      5
-------
```

7 ones – 2 ones
= 5 ones

```
  5 ?3 7
– 2  7 2
--------
       5
--------
```

We can't subtract 7 tens from 3 tens.
We regroup the hundreds and tens.

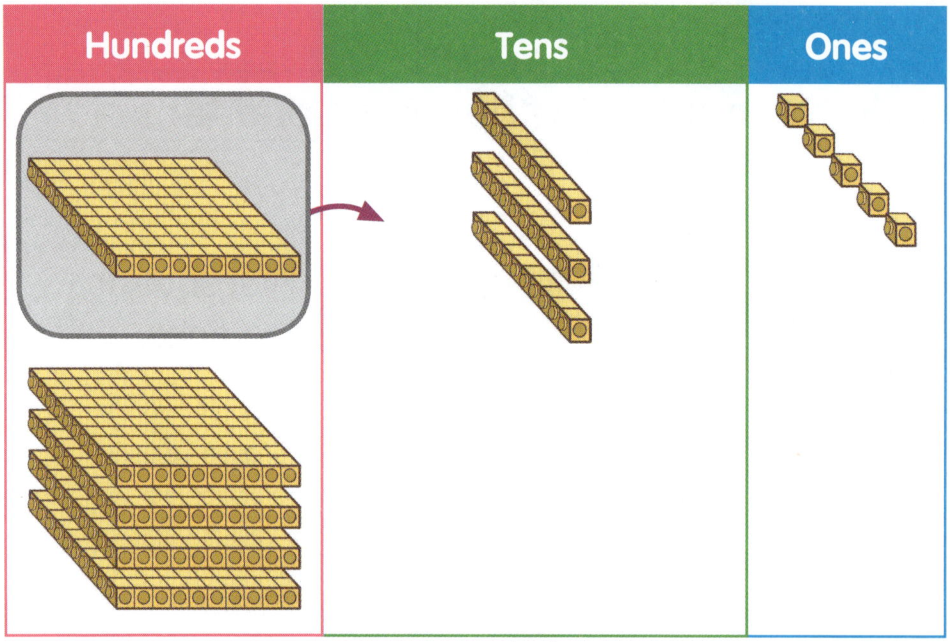

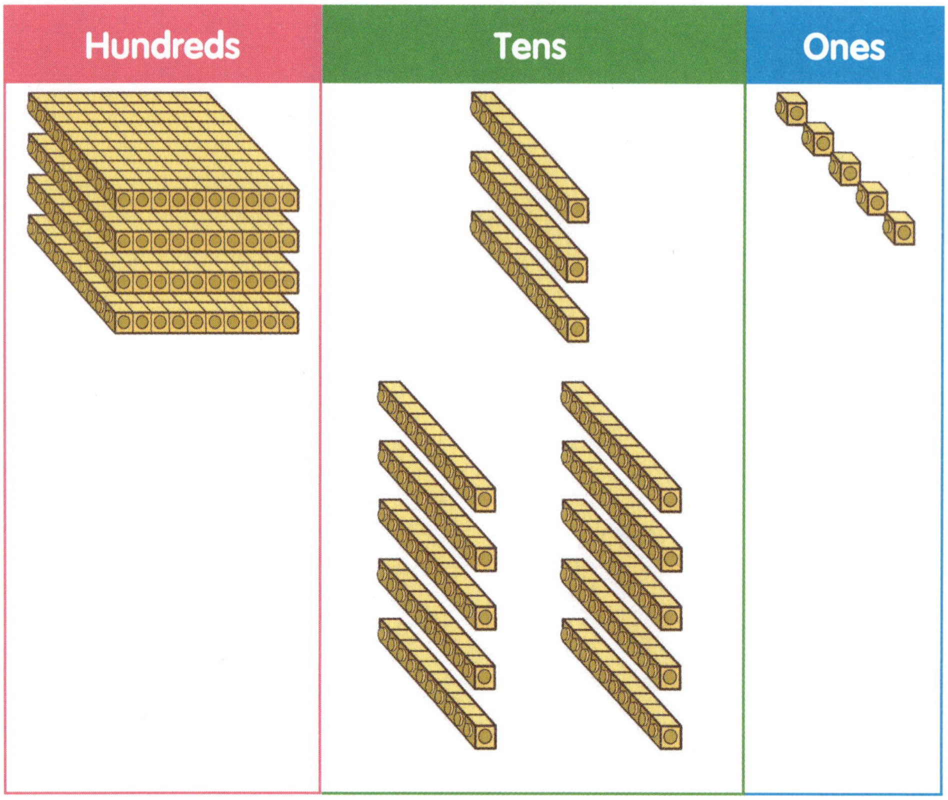

Regroup the hundreds and tens.

$$\begin{array}{r} {}^{4}\cancel{5}\ {}^{1}3\ 7 \\ -\ 2\ \ 7\ 2 \\ \hline 5 \\ \hline \end{array}$$

5 hundreds
3 tens
= 4 hundreds
13 tens

Remember to regroup when you don't have enough to subtract.

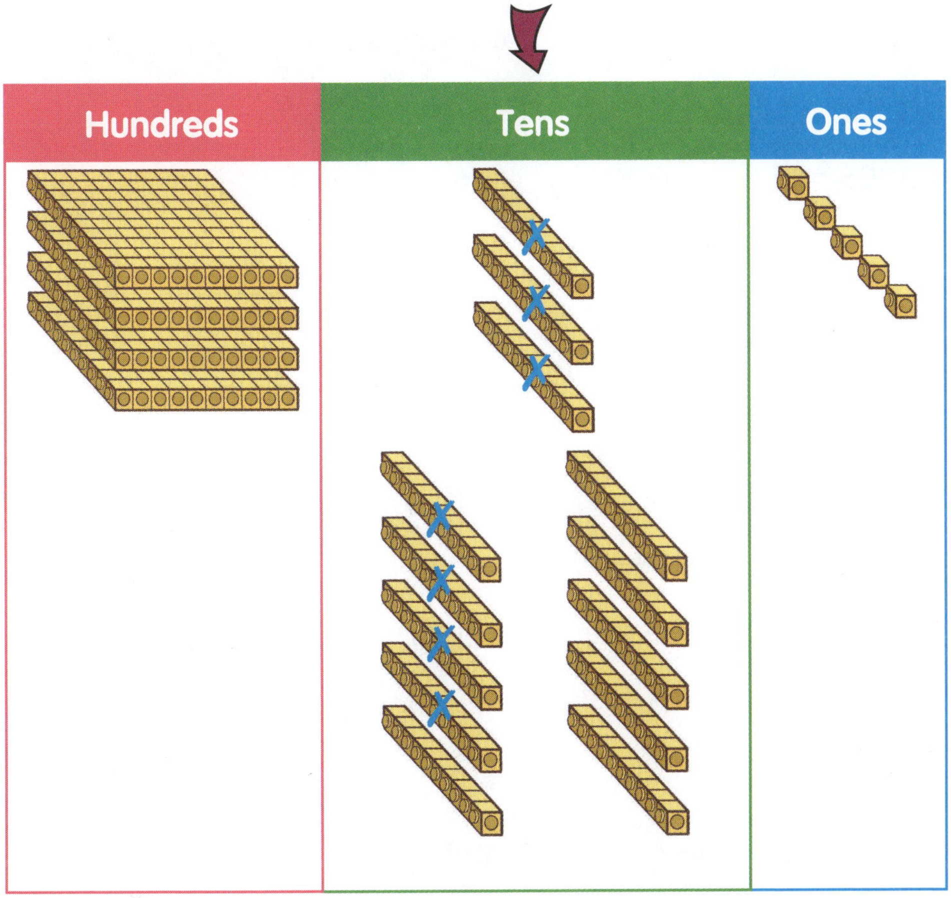

Then subtract the tens.

$$\begin{array}{r} {}^{4}\not{5}\ {}^{1}3\ 7 \\ -\ 2\ \ 7\ 2 \\ \hline 6\ 5 \\ \hline \end{array}$$

13 tens – 7 tens
= 6 tens

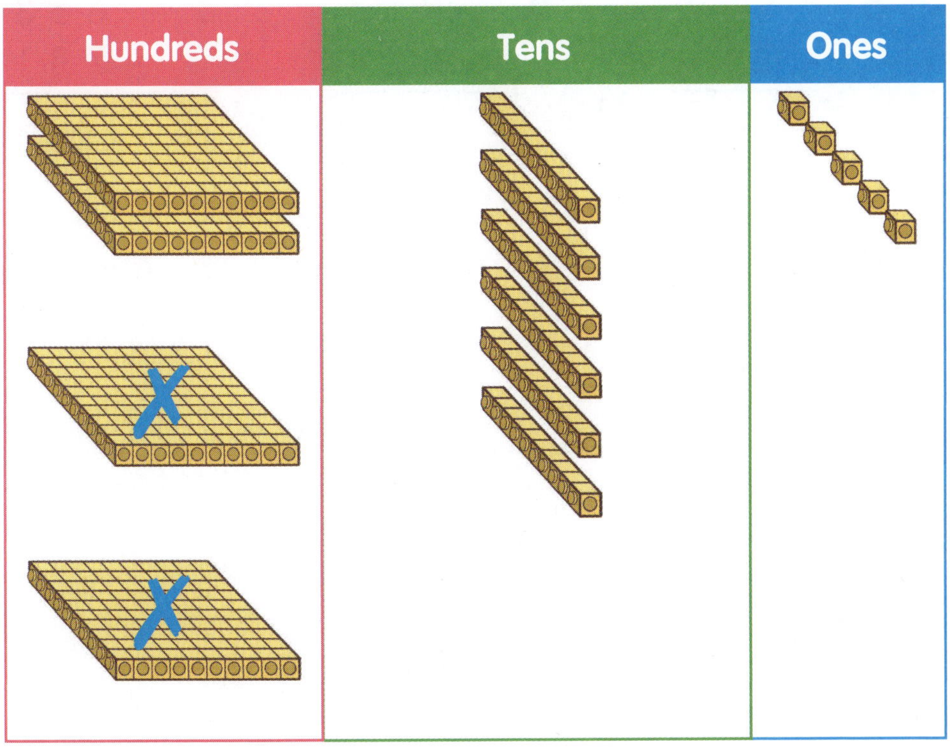

Finally subtract the hundreds.

$$\begin{array}{r} {}^{4}\not{5}\ {}^{1}3\ 7 \\ -\ 2\ \ 7\ 2 \\ \hline 2\ \ 6\ 5 \\ \hline \end{array}$$

4 hundreds
– 2 hundreds
= 2 hundreds

265

537 – 272 = 265

2 719 – 383 = ?

```
  7 1 9
– 3 8 3
-------
  [   ]
-------
```

First subtract the ones.

9 ones – 3 ones = ☐ ones

Regroup the hundreds and tens.

7 hundreds 1 ten = 6 hundreds ☐ tens

Then subtract the tens.

☐ tens – ☐ tens = ☐ tens

Finally subtract the hundreds.

6 hundreds – 3 hundreds = ☐ hundreds

719 – 383 = ☐

3 Subtract. Use place value charts to help you.

Example

$$\begin{array}{r} {}^{3}\not{4}\,{}^{1}2\,8 \\ -\ 1\,5\,1 \\ \hline 2\,7\,7 \\ \hline \end{array}$$

a
$$\begin{array}{r} 6\,4\,7 \\ -\ 2\,6\,7 \\ \hline \square \\ \hline \end{array}$$

b
$$\begin{array}{r} 9\,1\,5 \\ -\ 8\,2\,4 \\ \hline \square \\ \hline \end{array}$$

c
$$\begin{array}{r} 8\,5\,3 \\ -\ 7\,9\,1 \\ \hline \square \\ \hline \end{array}$$

d
$$\begin{array}{r} 3\,3\,6 \\ -\ 1\,5\,4 \\ \hline \square \\ \hline \end{array}$$

e 589 – 493

f 604 – 311

4 Solve these word problems.

a Miya has 235 stickers.
Farha has 153 fewer stickers than Miya.
How many stickers does Farha have?

b A baker makes 306 rolls.
She sells 256 rolls.
How many rolls are left?

Game

5 Break a square!

How to play:

1 Each player gets 1 .

2 Swap the for 9 and 10 .

3 Roll two dice. Take away this number of from your and .

4 Take turns to play. You can swap 1 for 10 .

The first player to take away all their and wins!

Practice Book 2A, pp.47 and 49

Let's Learn!

Subtraction with regrouping the hundreds, tens and ones

1 432 – 178 = ?

432

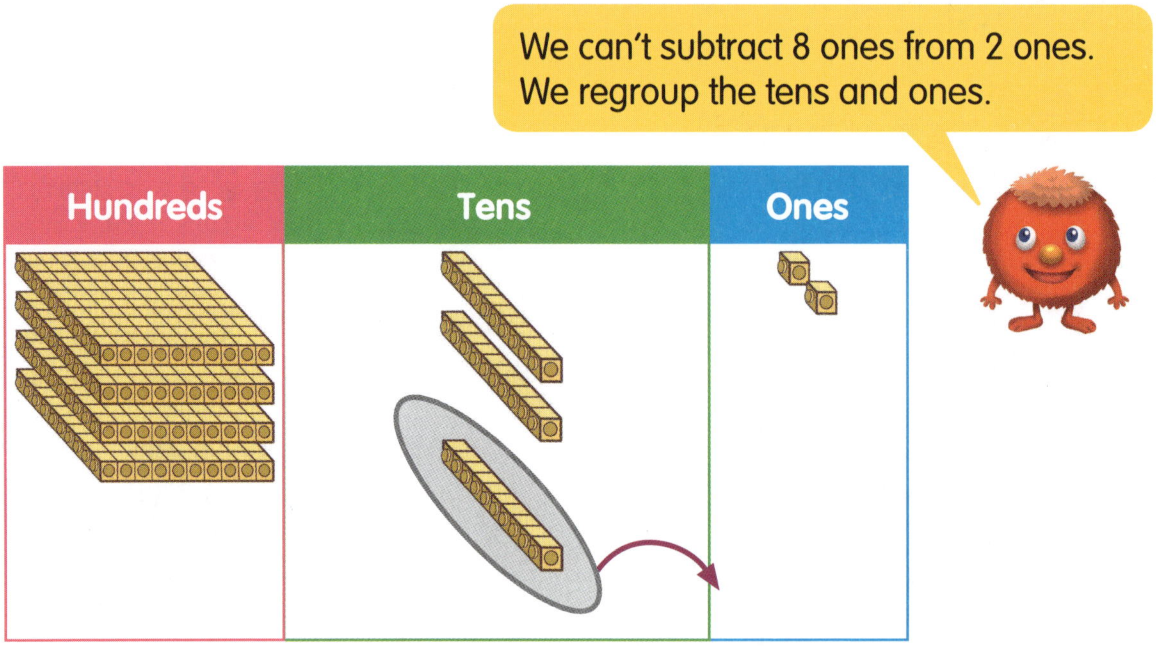

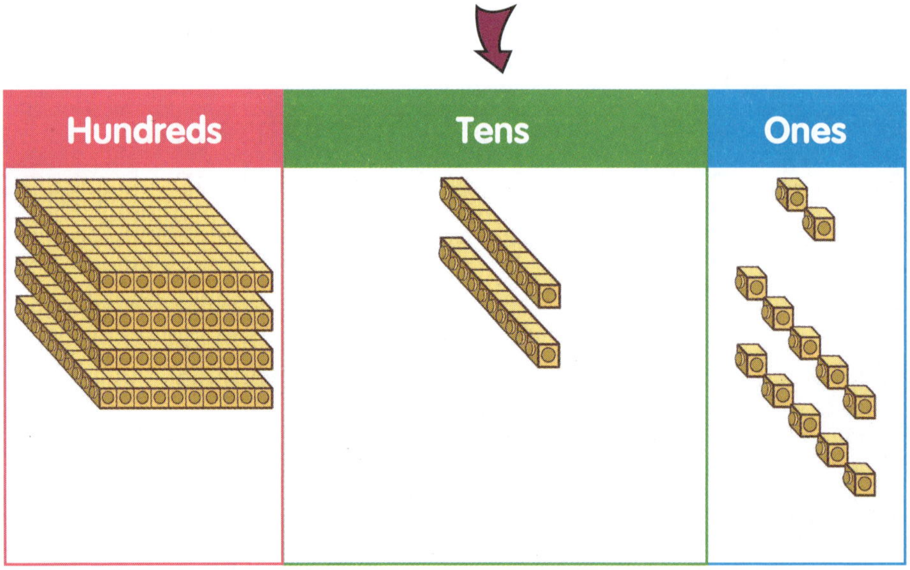

Regroup the tens and ones.

```
   4 ²3̶ ¹2
 – 1  7  8
 _________

 _________
```

3 tens 2 ones
= 2 tens 12 ones

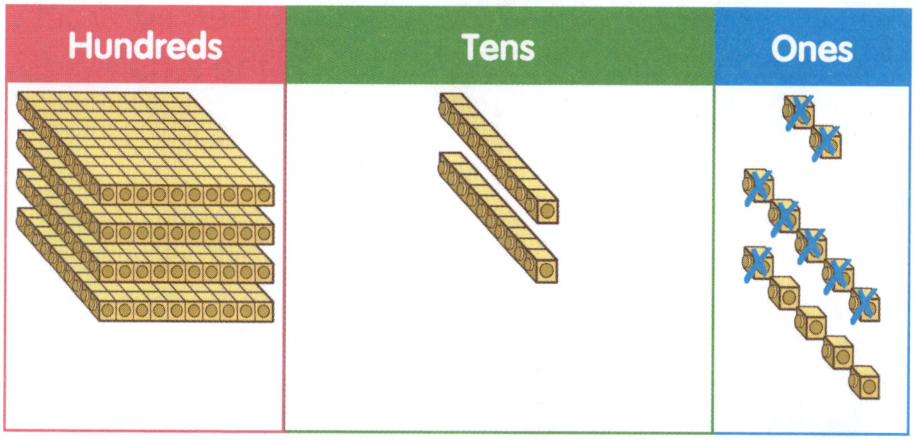

First subtract the ones.

$$\begin{array}{rrr} 4 & {}^{2}\not{3} & {}^{1}2 \\ -\ 1 & 7 & 8 \\ \hline & & 4 \end{array}$$

12 ones – 8 ones
= 4 ones

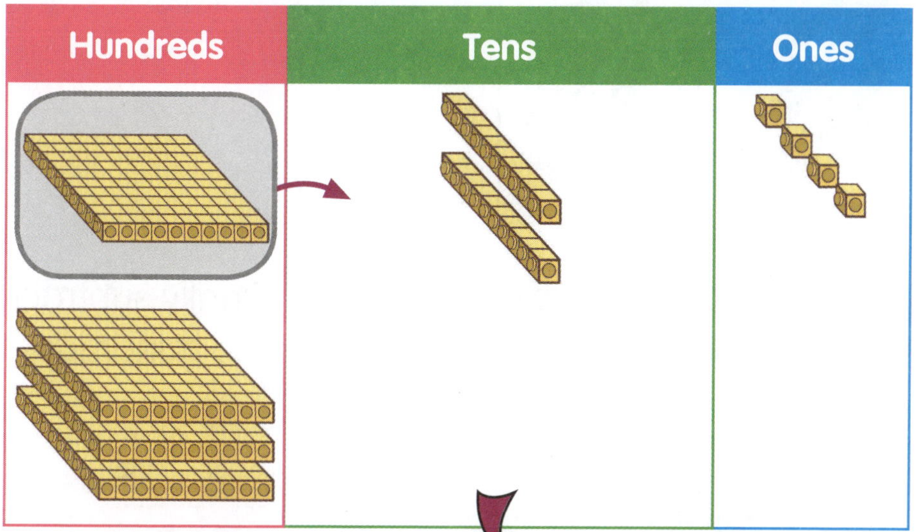

We can't subtract 7 tens from 2 tens. We regroup the hundreds and tens.

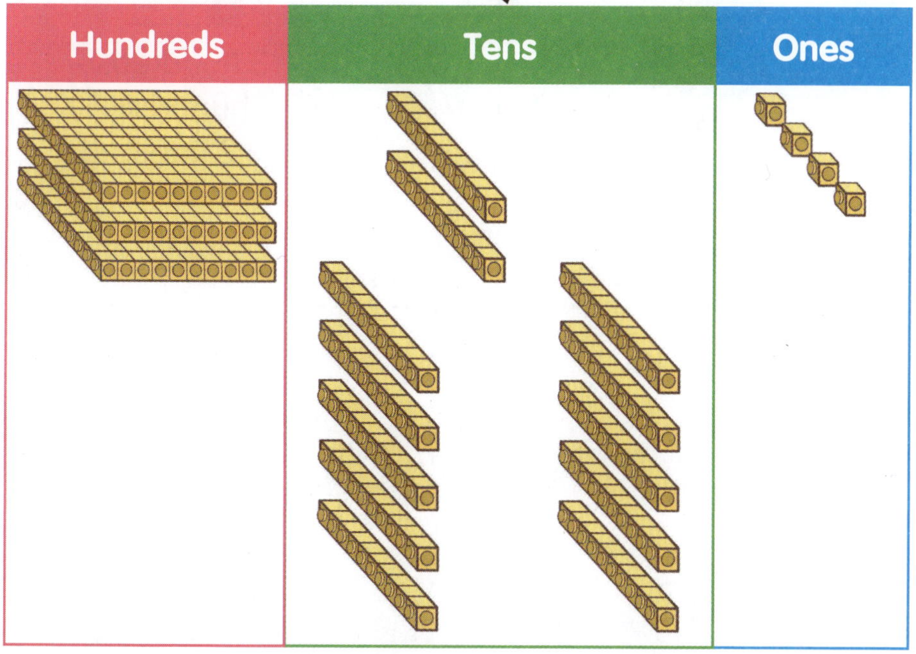

Regroup the hundreds and tens.

$$\begin{array}{rrr} {}^{3}\not{4} & {}^{12}\not{3} & {}^{1}2 \\ -\ 1 & 7 & 8 \\ \hline & & 4 \end{array}$$

4 hundreds 2 tens
= 3 hundreds
12 tens

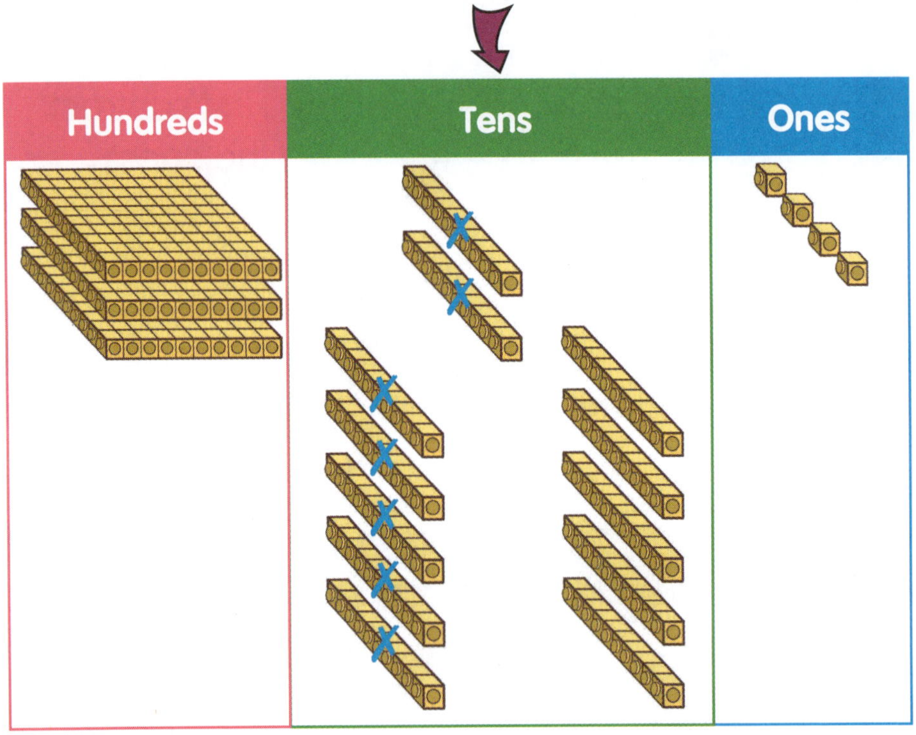

Then subtract the tens.

	$^{3}\not{4}$	$^{12}\not{3}$	$^{1}2$
−	1	7	8
		5	4

12 tens – 7 tens
= 5 tens

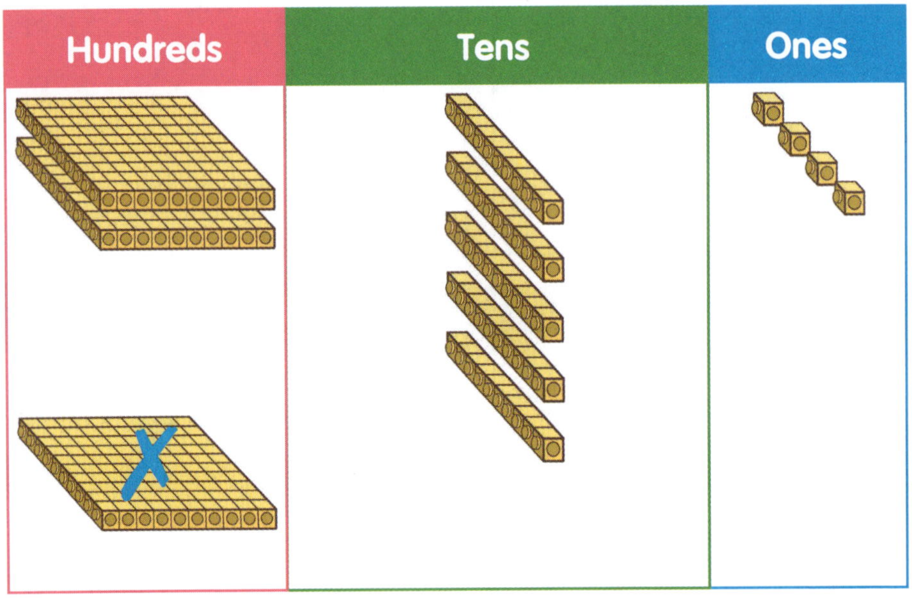

254

Finally subtract the hundreds.

	$^{3}\not{4}$	$^{12}\not{3}$	$^{1}2$
−	1	7	8
	2	5	4

3 hundreds –
1 hundred
= 2 hundreds

432 – 178 = 254

2 235 – 149 = ?

Write 235 – 149 in this way.
Then subtract.

```
  2 3 5
– 1 4 9
-------
  [   ]
-------
```

Regroup the tens and ones.

3 tens 5 ones = 2 tens [ ] ones

First subtract the ones.

[ ] ones – [ ] ones = [ ] ones

Regroup the hundreds and tens.

2 hundreds 2 tens = 1 hundred [ ] tens

Then subtract the tens.

[ ] tens – [ ] tens = [ ] tens

Finally subtract the hundreds.

1 hundred – 1 hundred = [ ] hundreds

235 – 149 = [ ]

3 Subtract the numbers.
Use place value charts to help you.

Example

```
  ³4̸ ¹⁰1̸ ¹5
–  2  6  7
----------
   1  4  8
```

a

```
  5 3 2
– 3 7 9
-------
  [   ]
```

b

```
  6 7 3
– 1 9 8
-------
  [   ]
```

c

```
  8 2 4
– 5 6 8
-------
  [   ]
```

d 812 – 238 **e** 673 – 498 **f** 317 – 289

4 Solve this word problem.

There are 612 boys in a school.
There are 138 fewer girls in the school.
How many girls are there?

Practice Book 2A, pp.51 and 53

Let's Learn!

Subtraction with numbers that have zeros

1 200 – 18 = ?

200

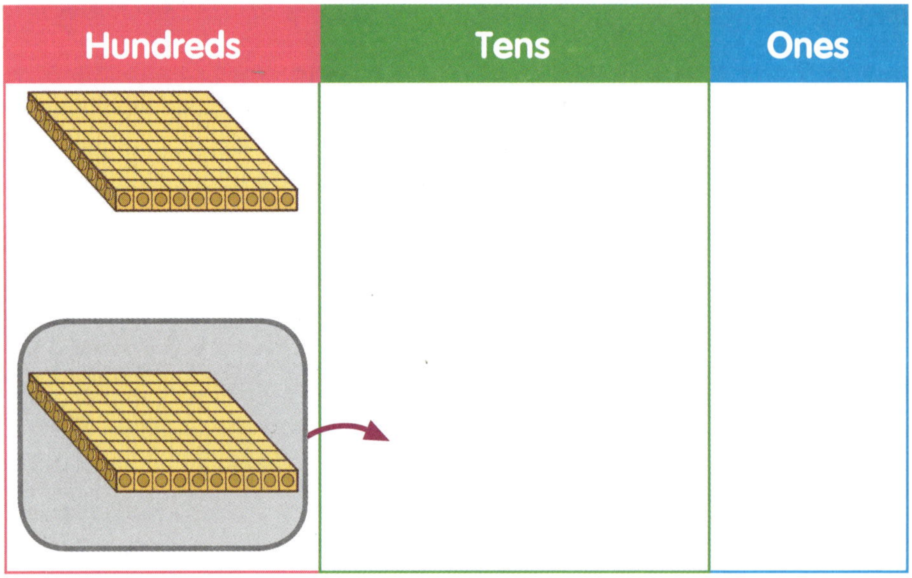


```
 ¹2̶ ¹0  0
–     1  8
_________

_________
```

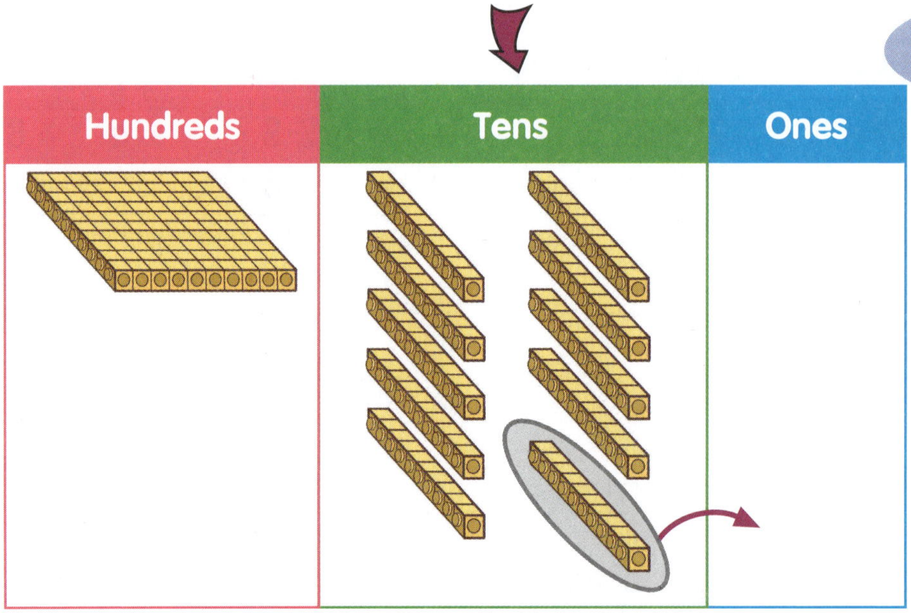


```
 ¹2̶ ⁹¹0̶ ¹0
–       1  8
___________

___________
```

2 hundreds = 1 hundred 10 tens
= 1 hundred 9 tens 10 ones

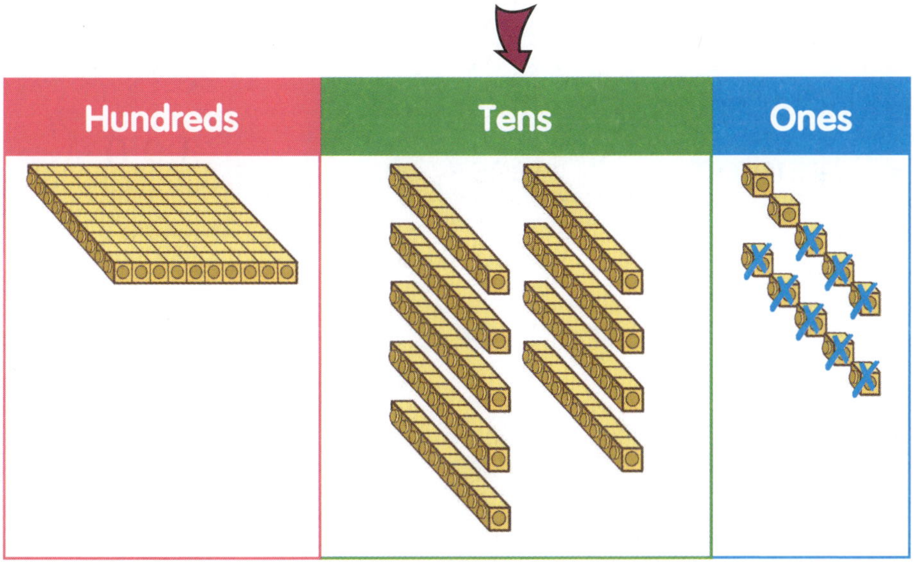

First subtract the ones.

$$\begin{array}{rrr} {}^{1}\cancel{2} & {}^{9}\cancel{{}^{1}0} & {}^{1}0 \\ - & 1 & 8 \\ \hline & & 2 \end{array}$$

10 ones – 8 ones
= 2 ones

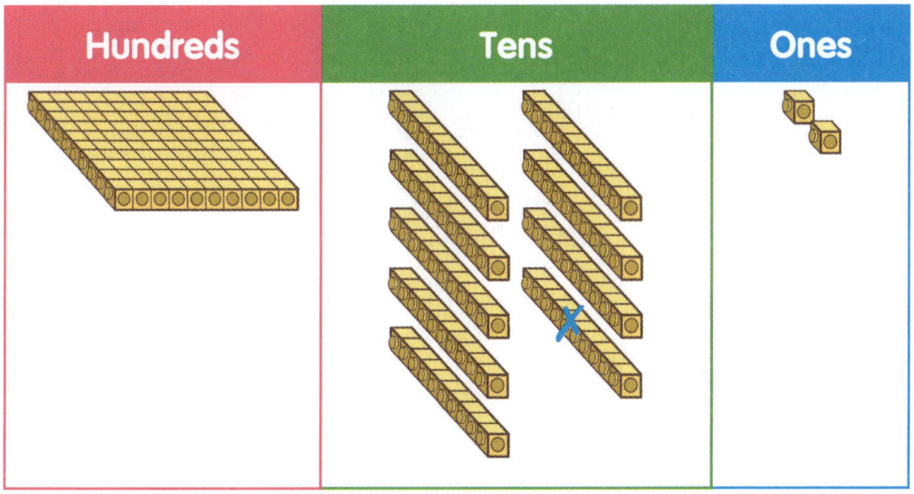

Then subtract the tens.

$$\begin{array}{rrr} {}^{1}\cancel{2} & {}^{9}\cancel{{}^{1}0} & {}^{1}0 \\ - & 1 & 8 \\ \hline & 8 & 2 \end{array}$$

9 tens – 1 ten
= 8 tens

182

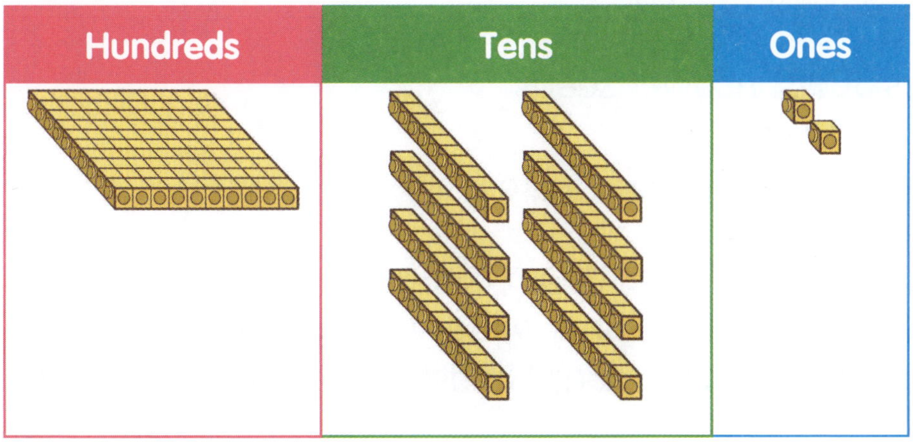

Finally subtract the hundreds.

$$\begin{array}{rrr} {}^{1}\cancel{2} & {}^{9}\cancel{{}^{1}0} & {}^{1}0 \\ - & 1 & 8 \\ \hline 1 & 8 & 2 \end{array}$$

1 hundred
– 0 hundreds
= 1 hundred

200 – 18 = 182

2 300 – 72 = ?

Regroup the hundreds, tens and ones.

3 hundreds = 2 hundreds [ ] tens

= 2 hundreds [ ] tens 10 ones

$$\begin{array}{r} 3\,0\,0 \\ -\quad 7\,2 \\ \hline \square \end{array}$$

300 – 72 = [ ]

3 Subtract the numbers. Use the place value charts to help you.

Example

$$\begin{array}{r} {}^{4}\not{5}\,{}^{9\,1}\not{0}\,{}^{1}0 \\ -\ 1\,6\,8 \\ \hline 3\,3\,2 \end{array}$$

a

$$\begin{array}{r} 1\,0\,0 \\ -\quad 9\,8 \\ \hline \square \end{array}$$

b

$$\begin{array}{r} 6\,0\,0 \\ -\ 3\,0\,8 \\ \hline \square \end{array}$$

c

$$\begin{array}{r} 9\,0\,0 \\ -\ 7\,3\,4 \\ \hline \square \end{array}$$

d 300 – 254

e 800 – 89

f 500 – 487

4 Solve these word problems.

a Jack has 200 stickers.
He gives away 24 stickers.
How many stickers are left?

b Millie has 300 sunflower seeds.
She plants 127 seeds.
How many sunflower seeds are left?

c Hardeep scores 400 points in a computer game.
His brother scores 189 points in the same game.
How many more points does Hardeep score than his brother?

Practice Book 2A, p.55

Put On Your Thinking Caps!

5

Find the missing number in each box.

$$\begin{array}{cccc} & 1 & 1 & 1 \\ + & \square & \square & \square \\ \hline & 3 & 3 & 3 \\ \hline \end{array} \qquad \begin{array}{cccc} & 4 & 3 & 2 \\ + & 4 & \square & 6 \\ \hline & 8 & 8 & 8 \\ \hline \end{array} \qquad \begin{array}{cccc} & 1 & 2 & \square \\ + & 3 & 4 & 5 \\ \hline & 4 & 6 & 8 \\ \hline \end{array}$$

$$\begin{array}{cccc} & & \square & \square \\ - & & & 1 \\ \hline & & 8 & 8 \\ \hline \end{array} \qquad \begin{array}{cccc} & \square & \square & \square \\ - & 4 & 4 & 4 \\ \hline & 4 & 4 & 4 \\ \hline \end{array} \qquad \begin{array}{cccc} & 6 & 5 & 4 \\ - & 2 & \square & 4 \\ \hline & 4 & 2 & 0 \\ \hline \end{array}$$

Practice Book 2A, p.57

Unit 3

Using Models: Addition and Subtraction

Let's Learn!

Let's Learn!

Simple word problems (1)

Adding sets of objects

1 Omar bakes 10 biscuits.
Ruby bakes 12 biscuits.
How many biscuits do they bake altogether?

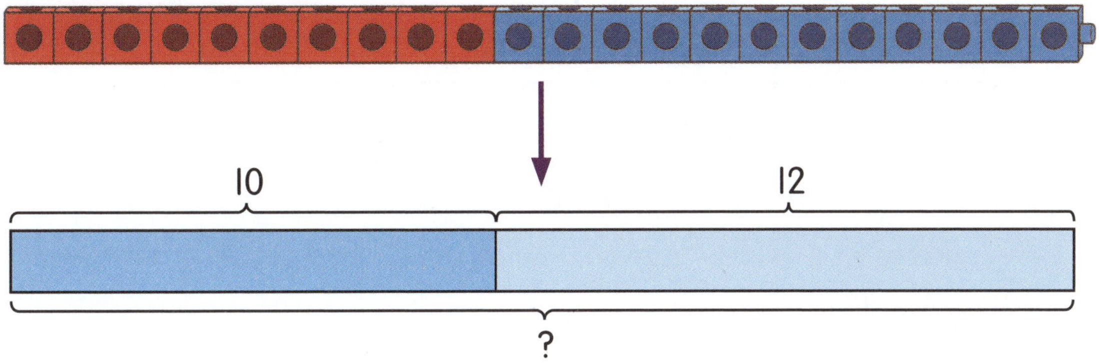

10 + 12 = 22

They bake 22 biscuits altogether.

2 Ella has 14 bracelets.
Ruby has 17 bracelets.
How many bracelets do they have altogether?

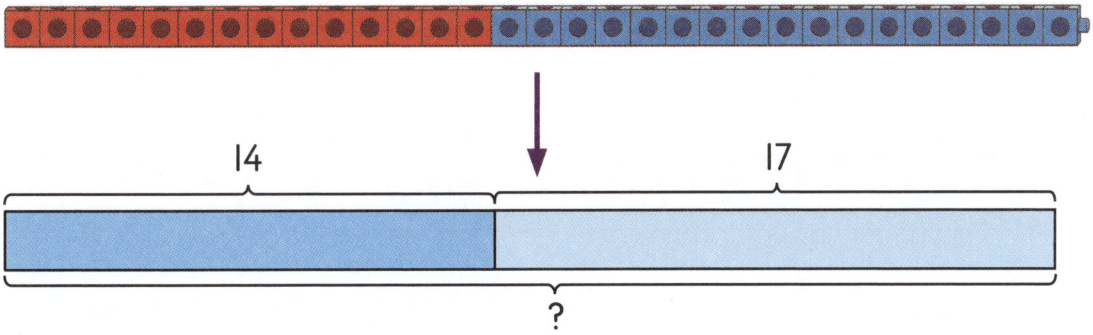

☐ + ☐ = ☐

They have ☐ bracelets altogether.

Finding 1 set of objects from a group

3 Hardeep buys large eggs and small eggs.
Altogether he buys 20 eggs.
There are 7 small eggs.
How many large eggs are there?

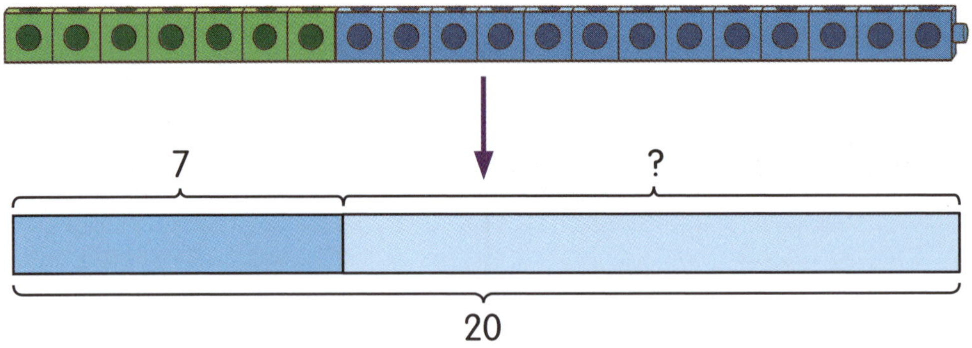

20 – 7 = 13

There are 13 large eggs.

4 Millie has a new fish tank.
She wants to put 21 fish in it.
Millie's mum gives her 15 fish.
She uses her pocket money to buy the rest.
How many fish does she buy?

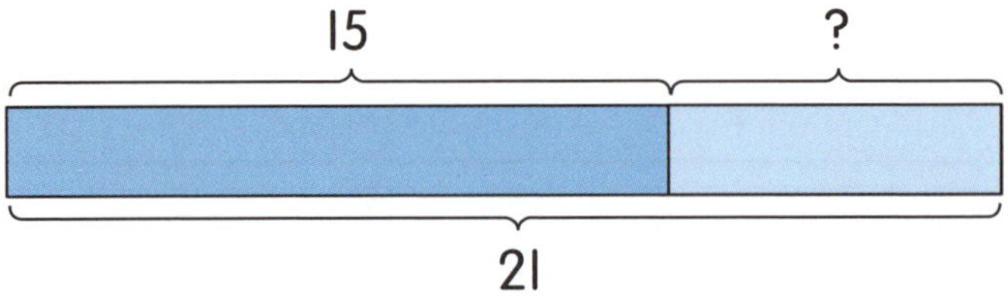

☐ – ☐ = ☐

Millie buys ☐ fish.

Activity

5 It's tale time!

1 Write your favourite name, your favourite toy and your favourite number on separate pieces of paper. Ask your friends to do the same.

2 Label three bags.

3 Put each piece of paper into the correct bag.

4 First pick a piece of paper from Bag 1.
Next pick another piece from Bag 2.
Then pick two pieces of paper from Bag 3.

Activity

5 Think of a word problem using the words and numbers.

6 Put the pieces of paper back into the correct bags.

7 Read out your word problem to your friends. Ask them to show your word problem by drawing models.

8 Take turns to pick pieces of paper from the bags and make word problems.

Example

Miya has 11 teddy bears.
3 of them are big.
The rest are small.
How many teddy bears are small?

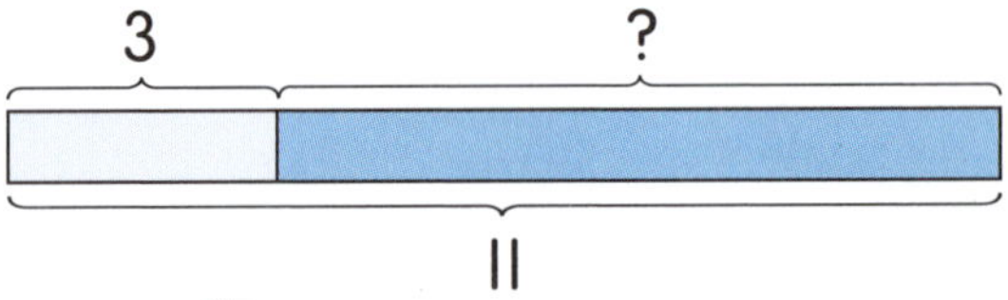

6 Draw models to solve the word problems.

a Millie's dad spends £225 on a new family tent.
He has £78 left.
How much did Millie's dad have at first?

b Mrs Green has £745 to spend on sports equipment.
She buys a trampoline for £257.
She spends the rest of the money on mats.
How much do the mats cost?

Practice Book 2A, p.65

Let's Learn!

Simple word problems (2)

Joining 1 or more sets to another set of objects

1 Miya has 87 beads.
Her friend gives her 78 more beads.
How many beads does Miya have now?

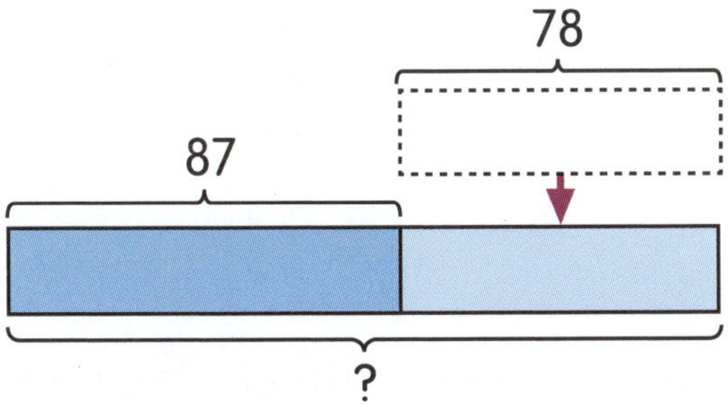

87 + 78 = 165

Miya has 165 beads now.

2 Tai has 9 football cards.
His cousin gives him 3 cards.
His sister buys him another 6 cards.
How many cards does Tai have altogether?

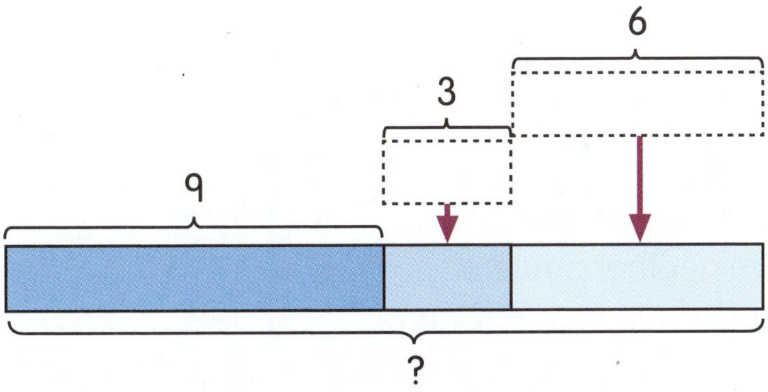

☐ + ☐ + ☐ = ☐

Tai has ☐ cards altogether.

Activity

3 We have more stories to tell.

1 You will need some objects from the classroom.

2 Think of a story using the objects that you have picked.

3 Use your friends' names and your favourite numbers in your story.

4 How many stories can you tell?
Show these stories with models.

Here's a story for you!

Jack has 8 rulers.
Millie gives him 9 more rulers.
Omar gives him another 5 rulers.
How many rulers does Jack have now?

Taking away 1 set

4 Millie has 98 flowers.
She gives some flowers away.
She has 28 flowers left.
How many flowers does she give away?

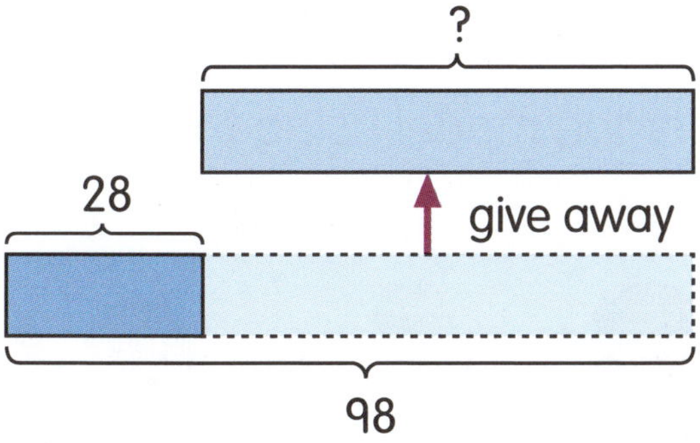

98 – 28 = 70

Millie gives away 70 flowers.

5 A farmer has 401 cows in a field.
He moves 212 cows to the milking shed.
How many cows are left in the field?

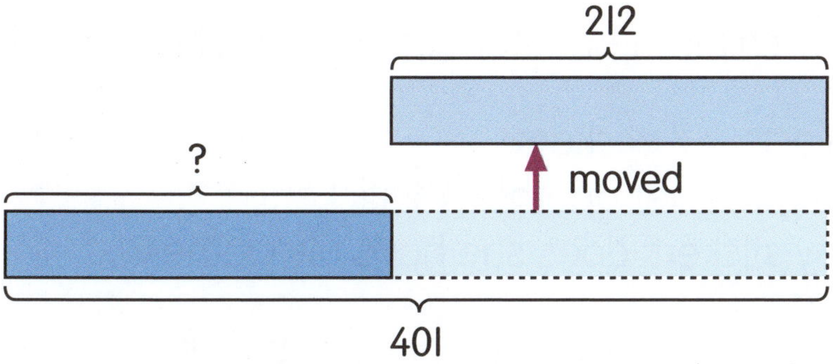

____ – ____ = ____

There are ____ cows left in the field.

Activity

6 **a** Look at the model.

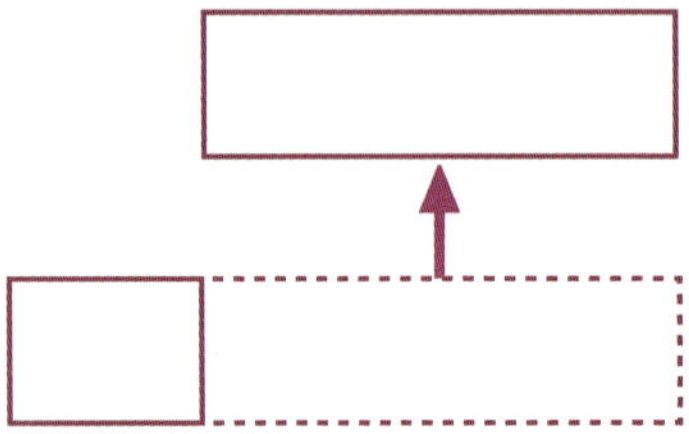

b Write a word problem for the model using the sets of items below.

eggs strawberries grapes tomatoes

c Ask your friends to solve your word problems.

7 Draw models to solve the word problems.

a There are 625 children in a school hall.
56 more children enter the hall.
How many children are there in the school hall now?

b Sarah collects 147 stickers.
Her friend gives her another 49 stickers.
How many stickers does she have altogether?

c Ruby picks 742 apples at her grandma's farm.
She sells 258 apples.
How many apples does Ruby have left?

Practice Book 2A, p.69

Let's Learn!

Simple word problems (3)

Comparing two sets

1. Mrs Williams has 213 chickens on her farm.
Mr Evans has 78 more chickens on his farm.
How many chickens does Mr Evans have on his farm?

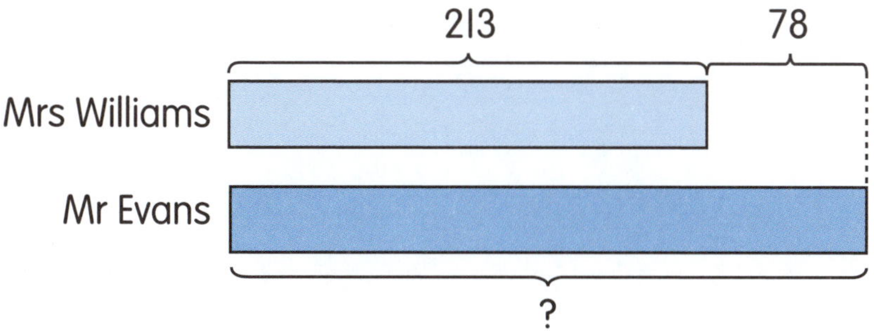

213 + 78 = 291

Mr Evans has 291 chickens on his farm.

2. 305 children go to the park on Saturday.
278 more children go to the park on Sunday than on Saturday.
How many children go to the park on Sunday?

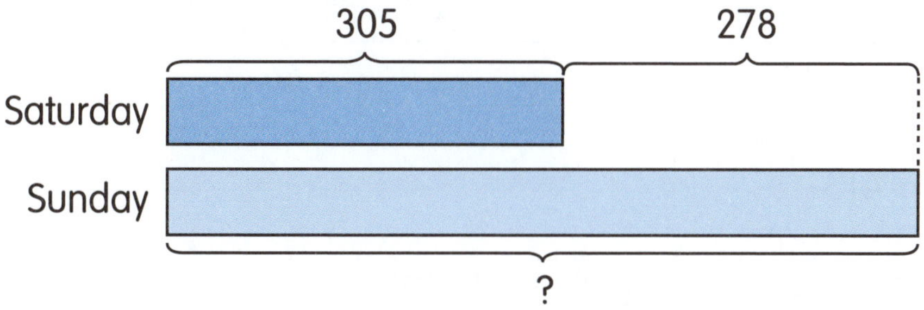

☐ + ☐ = ☐

☐ children go to the park on Sunday.

3 Ruby has £55.
Tai has £12 more than Ruby.
How much does Tai have?

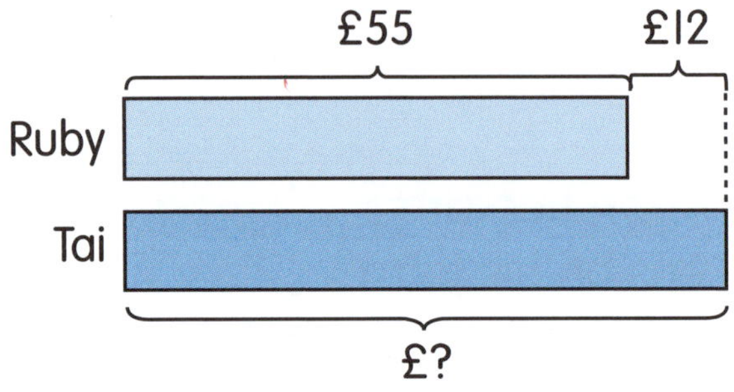

£ ☐ + £ ☐ = £ ☐

Tai has £ ☐.

4 459 children go swimming on Monday.
46 fewer children go swimming on Tuesday than on Monday.
How many children go swimming on Tuesday?

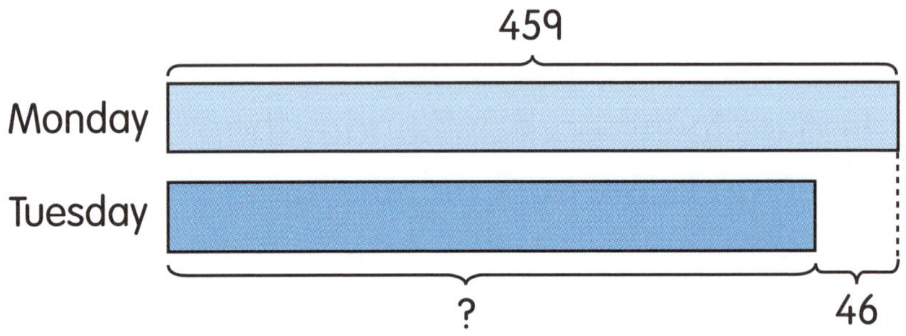

459 – 46 = 413

413 children go swimming on Tuesday.

5 Millie scores 824 points in a bowling competition.
Hardeep scores 157 points fewer than Millie.
How many points does Hardeep score?

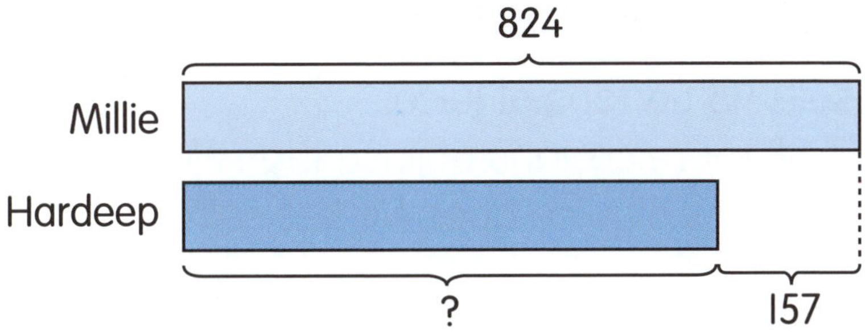

☐ – ☐ = ☐

Hardeep scores ☐ points.

6 Mr Green sells 300 newspapers on Monday.
He sells 126 more newspapers than Mr Jones on that day.
How many newspapers does Mr Jones sell?

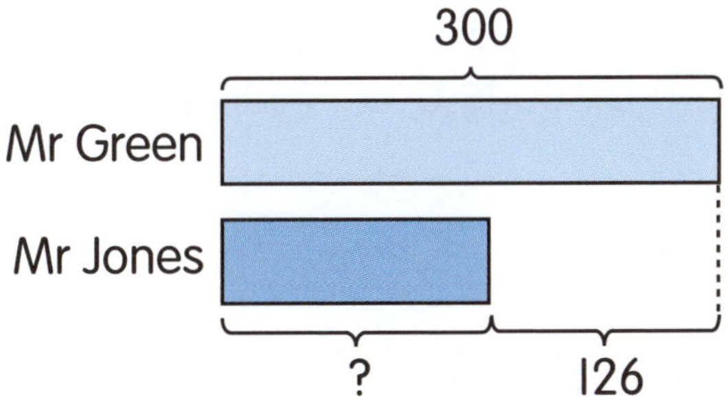

☐ – ☐ = ☐

Mr Jones sells ☐ newspapers.

Activity

7 Work in pairs.
Draw a model for each word problem and solve it.

a Mr Brown sells 95 cartons of juice.
Mr Lee sells 68 more cartons of juice than Mr Brown.
How many cartons of juice does Mr Lee sell?

b Ben can pack 150 balls in Box A.
He can pack 28 fewer balls in Box B than in Box A.
How many balls can Ben pack in Box B?

c Mrs Evans sells 56 fruit tarts.
Mr Cook sells 9 fewer fruit tarts than Mrs Evans.
How many fruit tarts does Mr Cook sell?

d Aisha makes 305 flapjacks for the school fair.
She makes 48 fewer chocolate chip biscuits than flapjacks.
How many chocolate chip biscuits does Aisha make?

e Jack and Tai collect shells.
Jack collects 210 shells.
Jack collects 34 fewer shells than Tai.
How many shells does Tai collect?

f Omar's mum spends £78 on a picnic table.
She spends £49 less than Peter's dad.
How much does Peter's dad spend?

Practice Book 2A, p.73

Let's Learn!

Two-step word problems

1 There are 26 boys and 19 girls in a hall.
7 children leave the hall.

a How many children are there in the hall at first?

b How many children are there in the hall at the end?

a

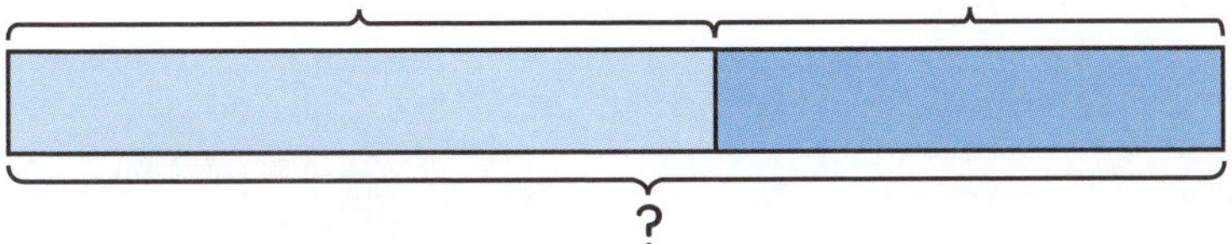

26 + 19 = 45

There are 45 children in the hall at first.

b

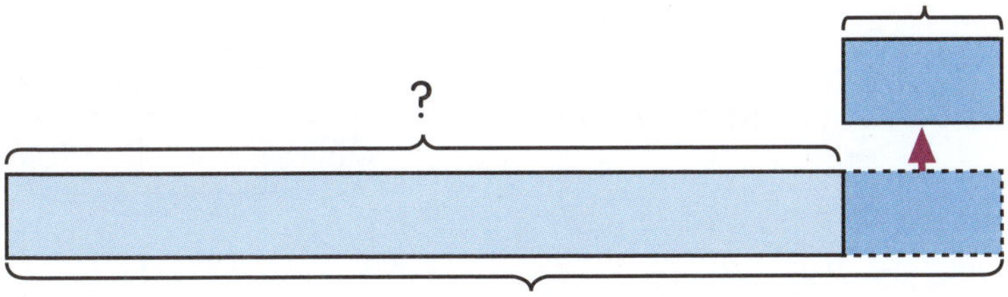

45 – 7 = 38

There are 38 children in the hall at the end.

2 Farha saves £341.
Ella saves £279 more than Farha.

a How much does Ella save?

b How much do they save altogether?

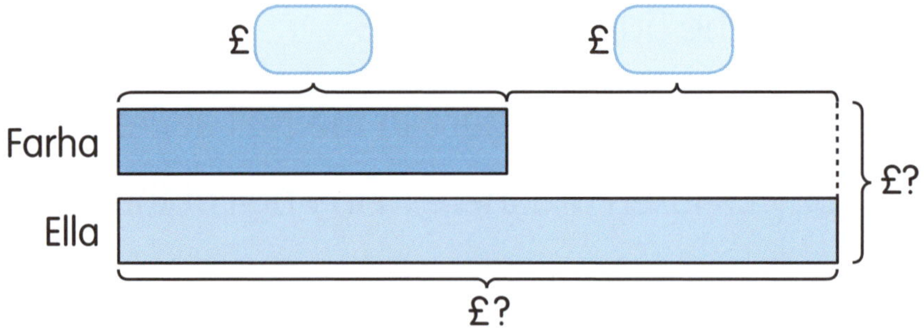

a £ ___ ◯ £ ___ = £ ___

Ella saves £ ___.

b £ ___ ◯ £ ___ = £ ___

They save £ ___ altogether.

3 There are 22 boys and 16 girls in Ruby's music class. There are 5 more children in Hardeep's music class than in Ruby's music class.

a How many children are there in Ruby's music class?

b How many children are there in Hardeep's music class?

a

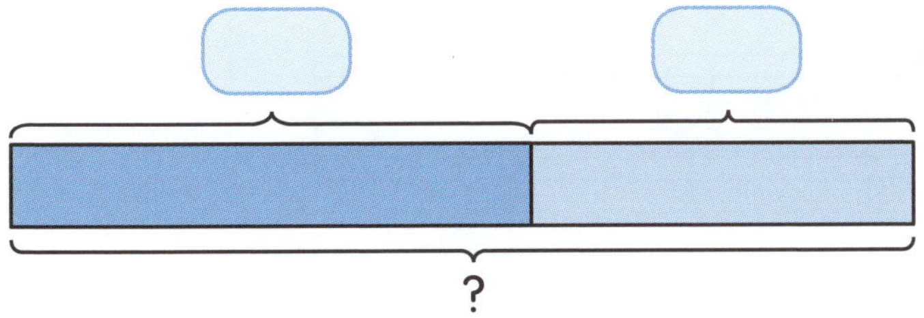

☐ ◯ ☐ = ☐

There are ☐ children in Ruby's music class.

b

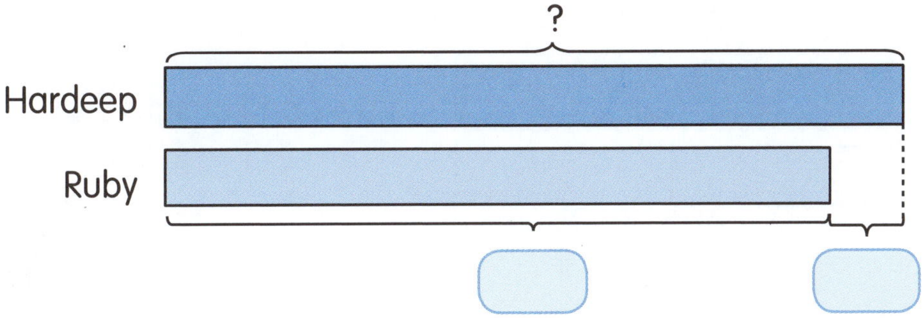

☐ ◯ ☐ = ☐

There are ☐ children in Hardeep's music class.

4 Peter has 264 English and French stamps altogether.
93 stamps are French stamps.

a How many English stamps does Peter have?

b How many more English stamps than French stamps does Peter have?

a

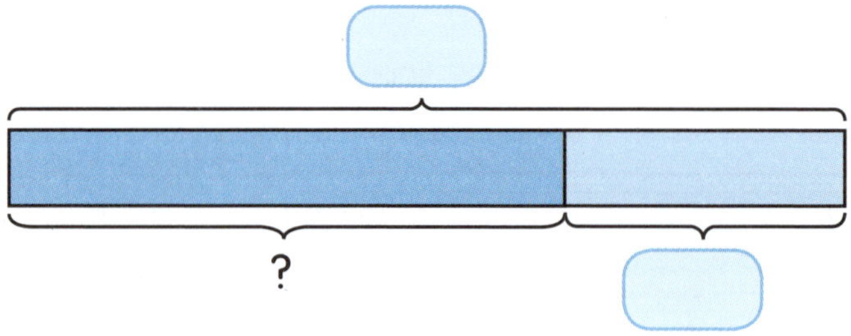

Peter has ___ English stamps.

b

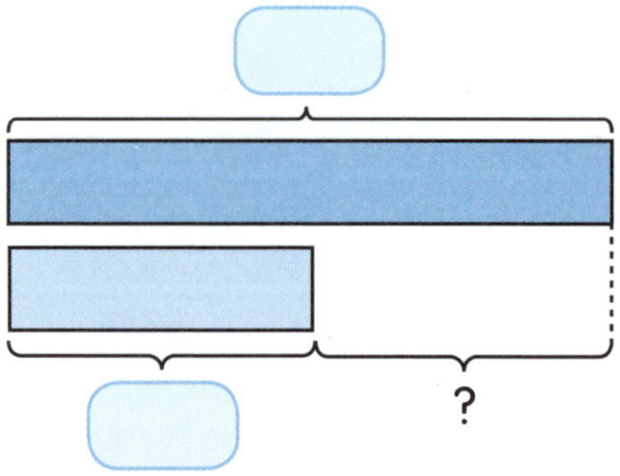

Peter has ___ more English stamps than French stamps.

5 Jack has 345 marbles.
He gives Tai 78 marbles.
Now Jack has 183 blue marbles and some red marbles.
How many red marbles does Jack have left?

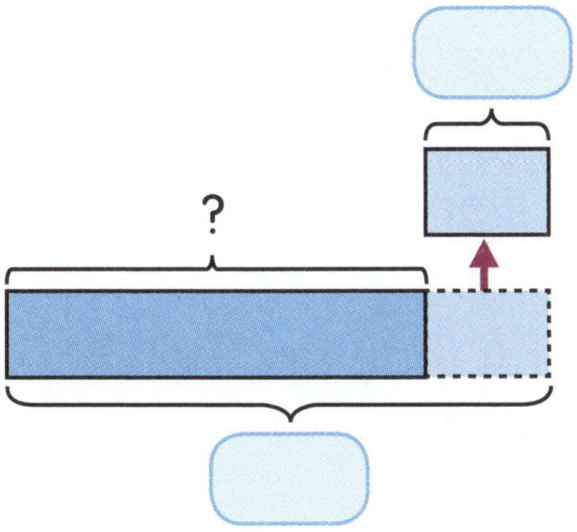

Jack has marbles left.

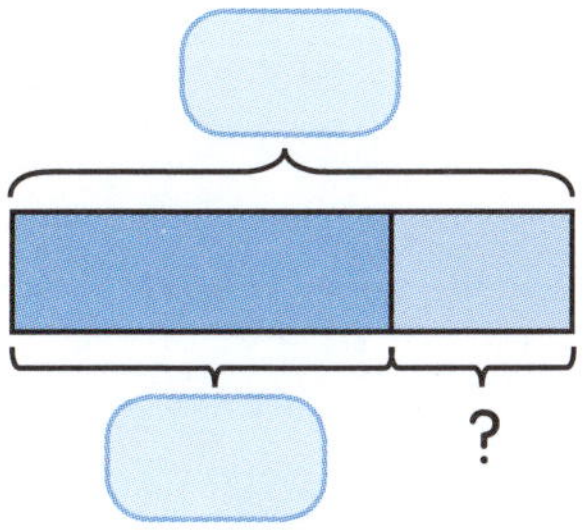

Jack has red marbles left.

6 Draw models to solve the word problems.

a Miya and Omar collect football cards.
Miya has 165 football cards.
She has 48 more cards than Omar.
How many cards do they have altogether?

b There are 56 comic books and 78 story books on Shelf A.
There are 39 fewer books on Shelf A than on Shelf B.
How many books are there on Shelf B?

c There are 264 boys in a school.
There are 58 fewer boys than girls.
178 girls have a brother.
How many girls do not have a brother?

Practice Book 2A, p.77

Let's Explore!

7

Hardeep, 327, give away, balls, Peter, 753 skateboards, Farha, altogether, how many, left, skipping ropes, Jack, 468, buys, hoops

Use the words and numbers to write

a two different word problems on addition

b two different word problems on subtraction

Unit 4 Multiplication and Division

Let's Learn!

How to multiply

How many cows are there?

There are two ways to find the number of cows.

Look at 1 and 2.

1. First count the number of groups.
   There are 3 groups.
   Then count the number of cows in each group.
   There are 5 cows in each group.

   $5 + 5 + 5 = 15$
   $3 \times 5 = 15$

   There are 15 cows altogether.

3 groups of 5 equal 15.
3 fives = 15

2. First count the number of items in each group.
   There are 5 cows in each group.
   Then count the number of groups.
   There are 3 groups.
   The number 5 is multiplied 3 times.

   $5 \times 3 = 5 + 5 + 5 = 15$

   There are 15 cows altogether.

5 times 3 is equal to 15.

3

How many plates are there? ____

How many muffins are there on each plate? ____

How many muffins are there altogether?

$3 \times$ ____ $=$ ____ or $2 \times$ ____ $=$ ____

There are ____ muffins altogether.

4 Miya buys 3 pizzas.
She cuts each pizza into 4 equal pieces.
How many pieces of pizza does Miya have?

Practice Book 2A, p.85

Let's Explore!

5 Look at the picture.

Make some multiplication stories about

a cakes

b drinks

c balloons

Example

There are 5 children. Each child has 2 hats.
There are 10 hats altogether.

Let's Learn!

How to divide

Sharing

1

Jack has 6 cherries.
He wants to divide the cherries into 2 equal groups.
How many cherries are there in each group?

$6 \div 2 = 3$

There are 3 cherries in each group.

Now he wants to divide them into
3 equal groups.

$6 \div 3 = 2$

There are 2 cherries in each group.

$6 \div 2 = 3$ and $6 \div 3 = 2$ are **division sentences**.

$6 \div 2 = 3$ says **six divided by two equals three**.

2 Peter has 15 biscuits.

a He gives an equal number of biscuits to each of his 3 friends. How many biscuits does each friend get?

15 ÷ 3 = ☐

Each friend gets ☐ biscuits.

b He gives an equal number of biscuits to each of his 5 friends. How many biscuits does each friend get?

15 ÷ ☐ = ☐

Each friend gets ☐ biscuits.

Grouping

3 Jack has 12 cards.

He divides the cards equally among his friends.

Each friend gets 4 cards. How many friends are there?

$12 \div 4 =$ ☐

There are ☐ friends.

4 Millie has 18 cards.

She gives the cards to some friends.

If each friend gets 3 cards, how many friends are there?

$18 \div 3 =$ ☐

There are ☐ friends.

Activity

5 Work in groups.

You will need 24 beads and some lolly sticks.

1 Divide the beads into equal groups of 2.
Write a division sentence.

Now make equal groups of

a 3 **b** 4 **c** 6 **d** 8 **e** 12

For each, write a division sentence.

2 Take 20 lolly sticks.
Make as many of the following shapes as possible.

a

b

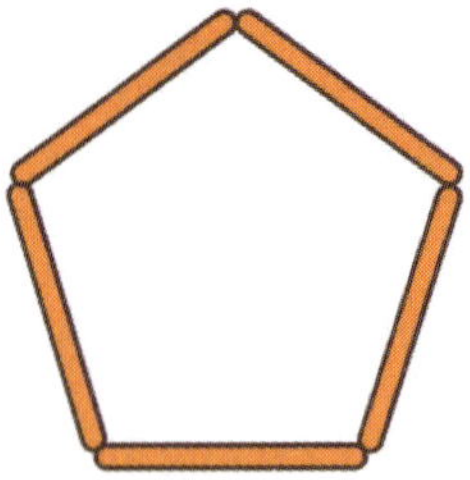

For each shape, write a division sentence.

3 Take 36 lolly sticks.
Make as many of the following shapes as possible.

a

b

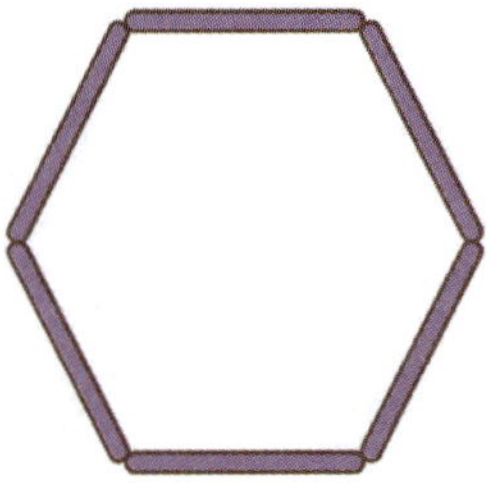

For each shape, write a division sentence.

Practice Book 2A, p.87

Let's Explore!

6 There are some animals in a garden.
Some of the animals have 2 legs.
The others have 4 legs.
Altogether the animals have 10 legs.

How many animals of each type are there?
You can have more than one answer.

Talk to your friends about your answers.

(Hint: Draw diagrams to help you.)

Put On Your Thinking Caps!

7 At the end of the first day,
this alien will split into two.
This means at the end of the first day
there will be two aliens.
At the end of the second day,
each of the two aliens will split into two.

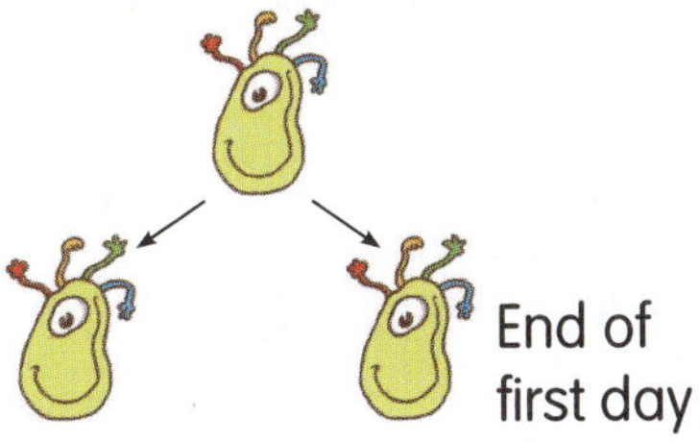

How many aliens will there be at the end of the second day?

Practice Book 2A, p.89
Practice Book 2A, p.90

Unit 5 Multiplying by 2 and 3

Let's Learn!

Multiplying by 2: skip-counting

1 There are 2 scooters in 1 group.
$1 \times 2 = 2$

How many scooters are there in 10 groups?

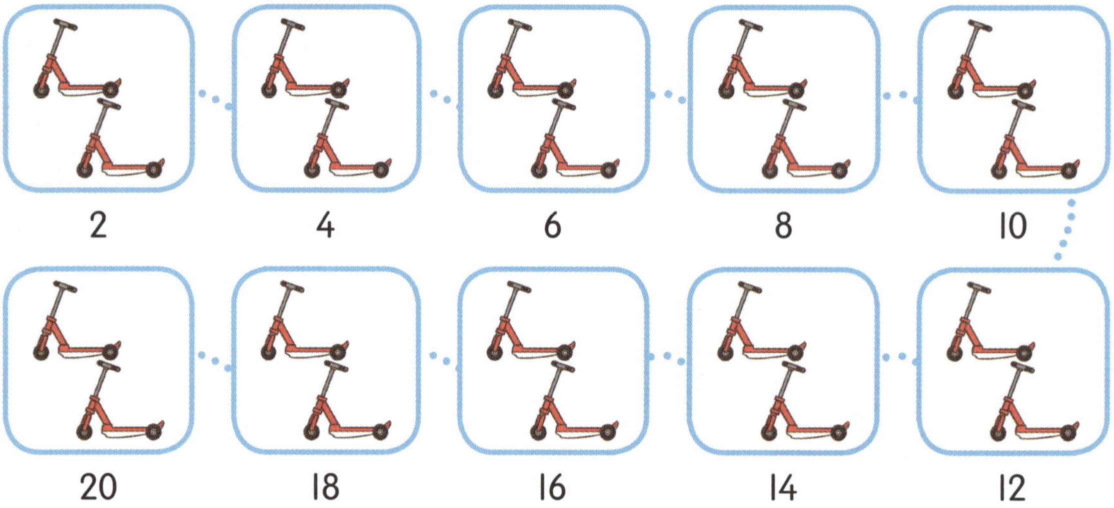

2, 4, 6, 8, 10, 12, 14, 16, 18, 20

$10 \times 2 = 20$

There are 20 scooters.

2 Jack has 7 bags.
There are 2 sandwiches in each bag.
How many sandwiches does he have altogether?

Jack has 14 sandwiches altogether.

3 Ella has 8 jars.
There are 2 marbles in each jar.
How many marbles does Ella have altogether?

___ × ___ = ___

Ella has ___ marbles altogether.

Activity

4 Crack the code on the wheel.

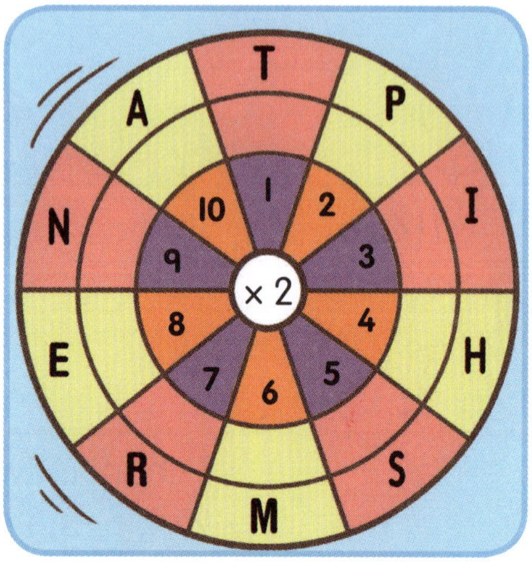

Copy and complete the multiplication sentences.

N $9 \times 2 =$ ☐

M $6 \times 2 =$ ☐

S $5 \times 2 =$ ☐

E $8 \times 2 =$ ☐

A $10 \times 2 =$ ☐

H $4 \times 2 =$ ☐

P $2 \times 2 =$ ☐

T $1 \times 2 =$ ☐

R $7 \times 2 =$ ☐

I $3 \times 2 =$ ☐

Match the letters to the answers.

☐	☐	☐	☐	☐	☐	☐
6	18	10	4	6	14	16

☐	☐	☐	☐	☐
12	20	2	8	10

Practice Book 2B, p.5

Let's Learn!

Multiplying by 2: using dot paper

1

Each sheep has 2 lambs.

How many lambs will 3 sheep have altogether?

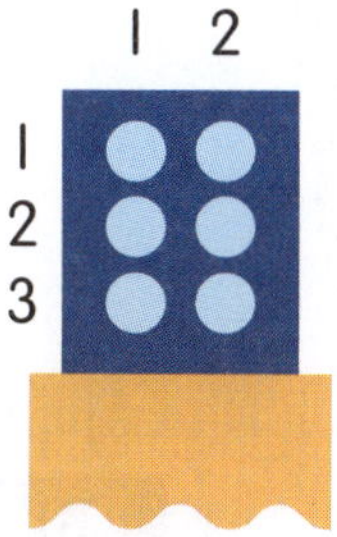

$3 \times 2 = 6$

3 sheep will have 6 lambs altogether.

2 Peter has 4 pairs of coloured pencils.
How many coloured pencils does he have altogether?

$4 \times 2 =$ ☐

Peter has ☐ coloured pencils altogether.

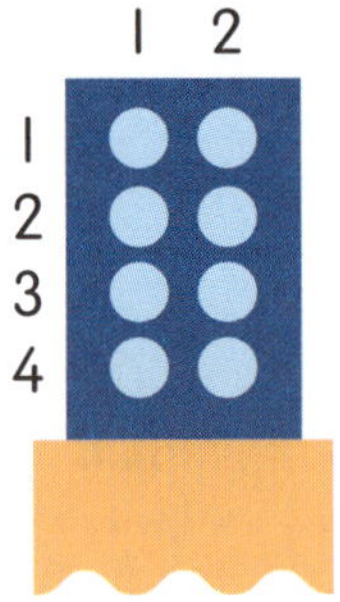

3 Each child collects 2 stamps.
How many stamps did the 5 children collect altogether?

$5 \times 2 =$ ☐

The 5 children collected ☐ stamps altogether.

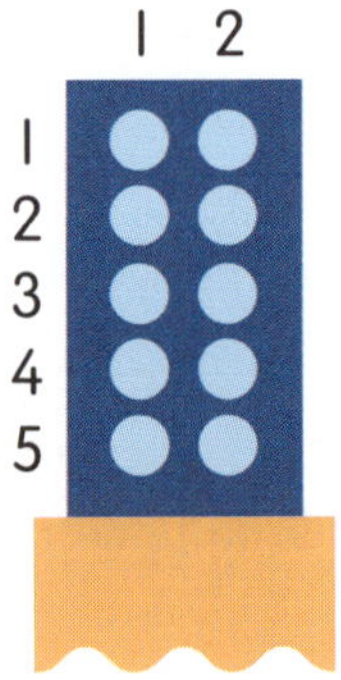

4 There are 6 pairs of socks on a washing line.
How many socks are there altogether?

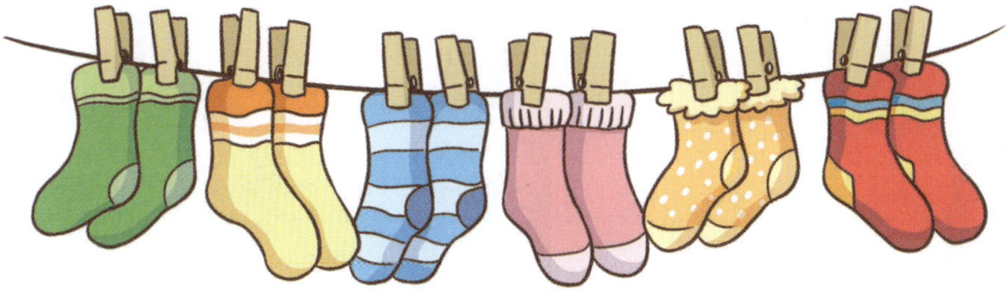

$6 \times 2 =$ ☐

There are ☐ socks altogether.

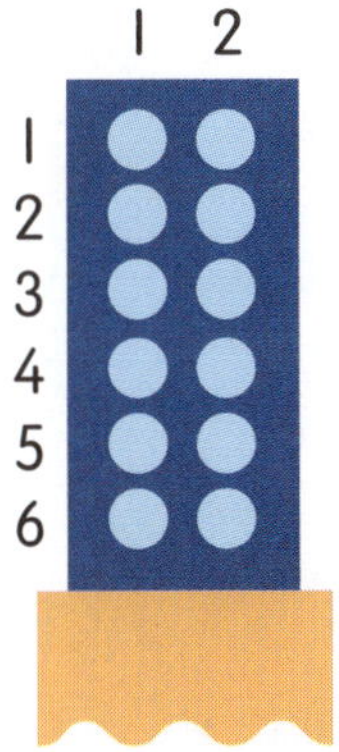

5 Short cuts!

a $6 \times 2 = ?$
Start with 5 groups of 2.

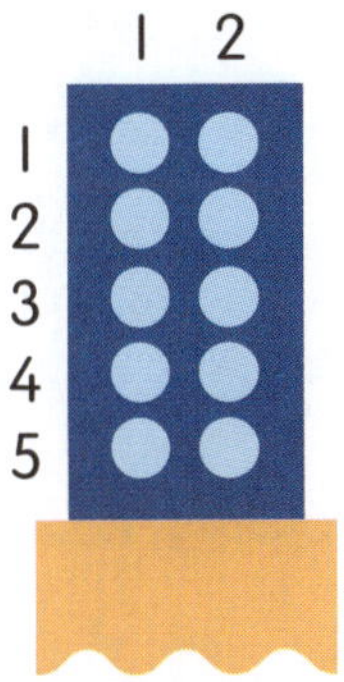

$5 \times 2 = 10$

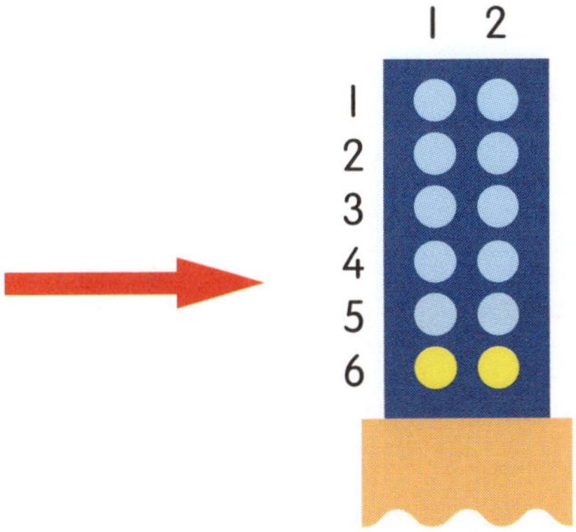

$6 \times 2 = 10 + 2$
$= 12$

Home Maths Use coins or stickers to help your child understand how to use the dot paper.

b $7 \times 2 = ?$

Start with 5 groups of 2.

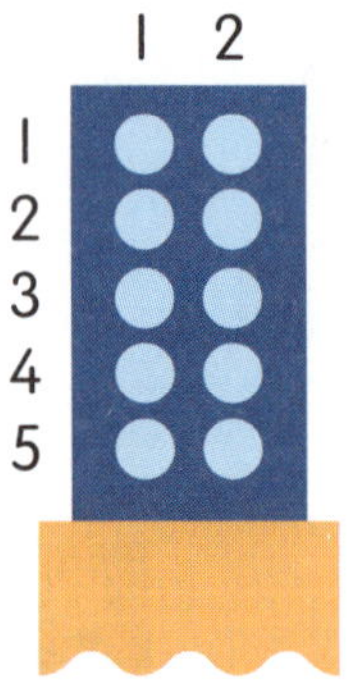

$5 \times 2 = 10$

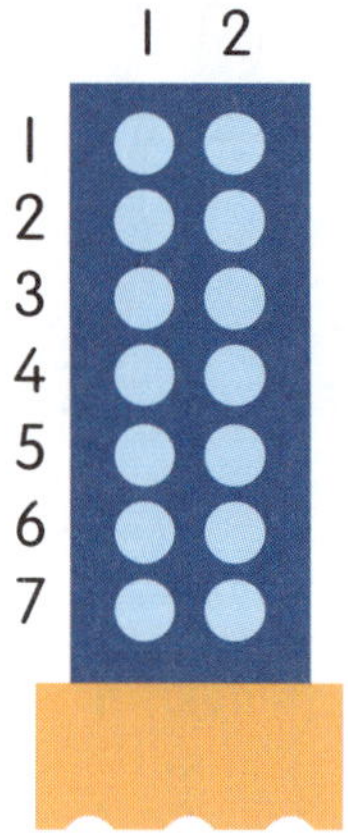

$7 \times 2 = 10 + \square$

$= \square$

c $9 \times 2 = ?$

Start with 10 groups of 2.

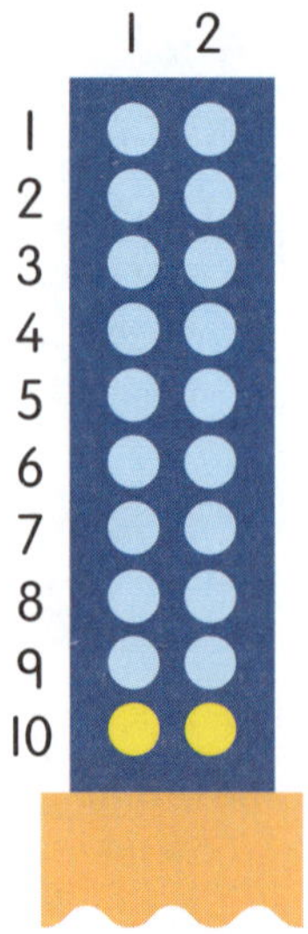

$10 \times 2 = 20$

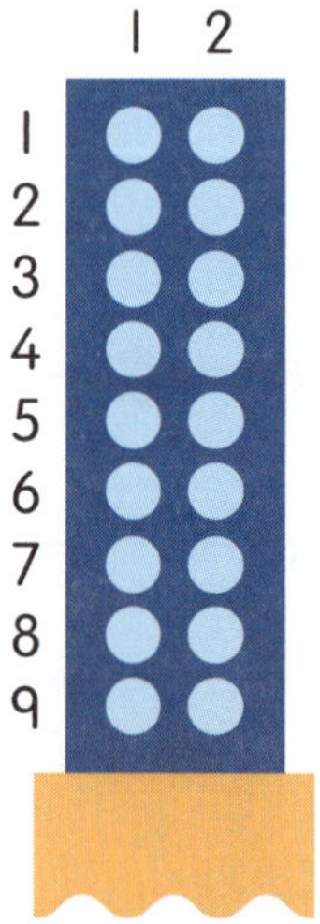

$9 \times 2 = 20 - 2$

$= 18$

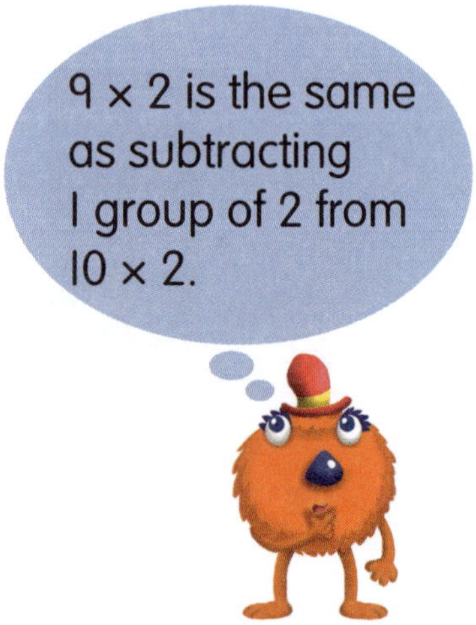

d $8 \times 2 = ?$
Start with 10 groups of 2.

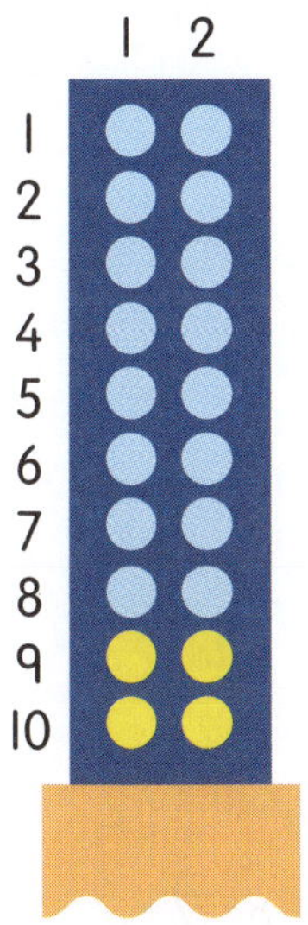

$10 \times 2 = 20$

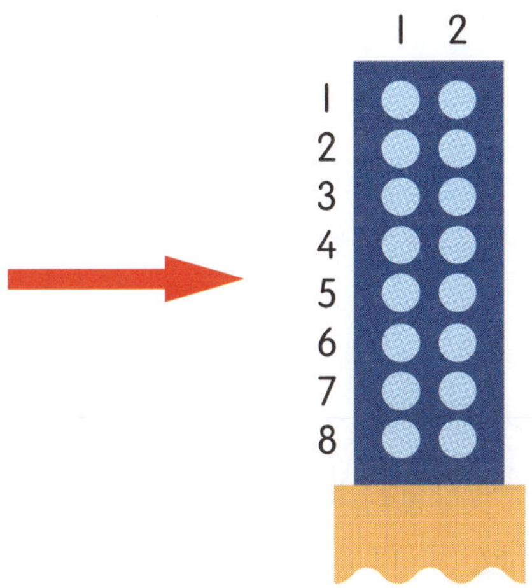

$8 \times 2 = 20 - $ ☐
$= $ ☐

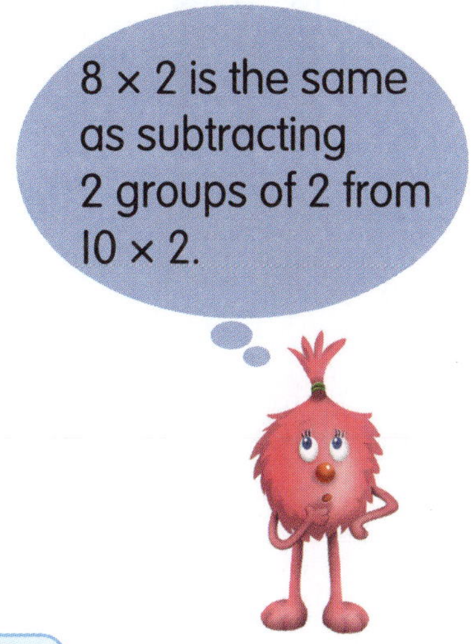

6 2 times table

1	×	2	=	2
2	×	2	=	4
3	×	2	=	6
4	×	2	=	8
5	×	2	=	10
6	×	2	=	12
7	×	2	=	14
8	×	2	=	16
9	×	2	=	18
10	×	2	=	20

7 $4 \times 2 = 8$

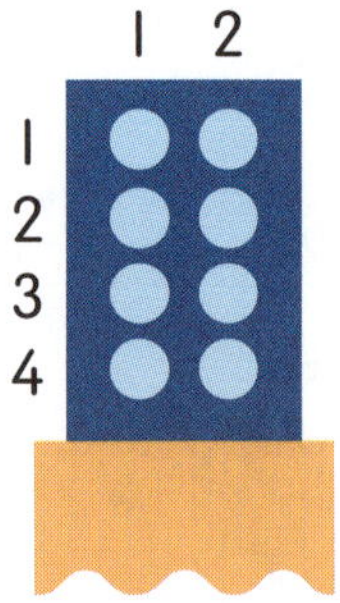

$2 \times 4 = 8$

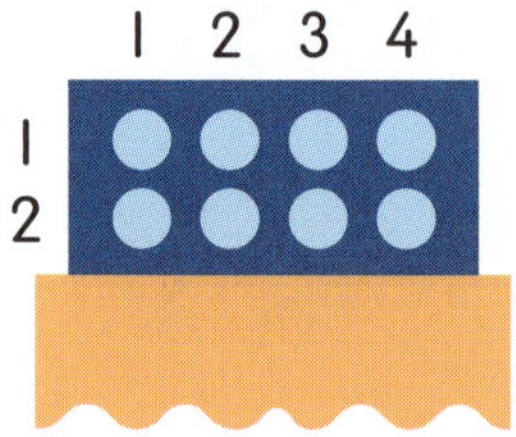

8 Find the missing numbers.
Use the dot paper to help you.

$\square \times \square = 14$ $\square \times \square = 14$

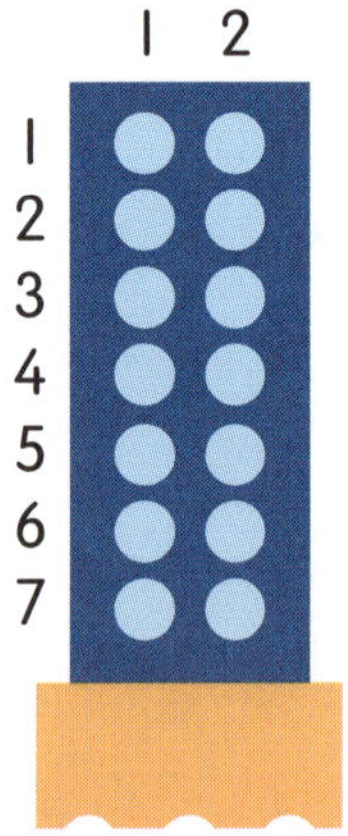

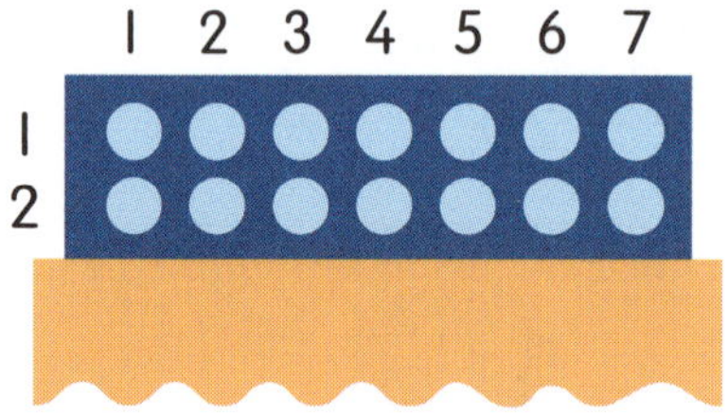

9 Answer these questions.

a $5 \times 2 = \square$ $7 \times 2 = \square + 4 = \square$

b $10 \times 2 = \square$ $9 \times 2 = \square - 2 = \square$

c $6 \times 2 = \square$ $2 \times 6 = \square$

d $8 \times 2 = \square$ $2 \times 8 = \square$

Practice Book 2B, p.7

Let's Learn!

Multiplying by 3: skip-counting

1 Millie has a bag of 3 biscuits.

$1 \times 3 = 3$

How many biscuits are there in 10 bags?

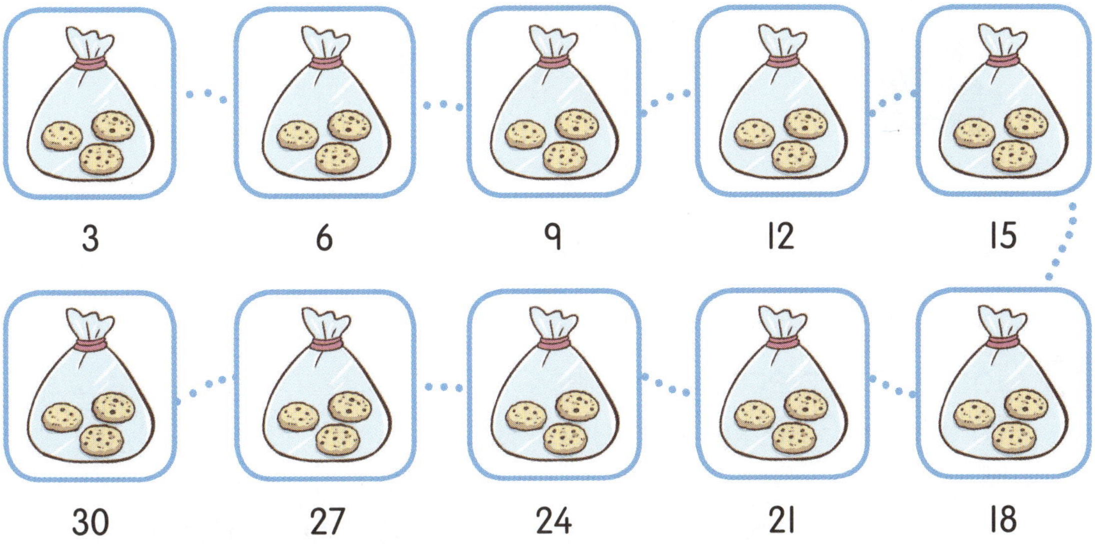

3, 6, 9, 12, 15, 18, 21, 24, 27, 30

$10 \times 3 = 30$

There are 30 biscuits.

2 Ruby has 4 plates.
There are 3 pears on each plate.
How many pears does she have altogether?

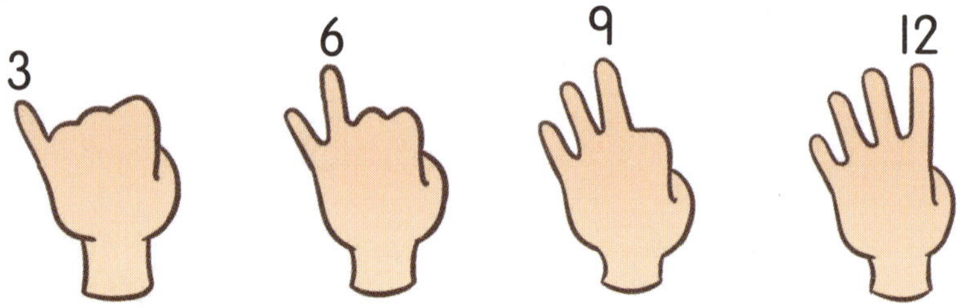

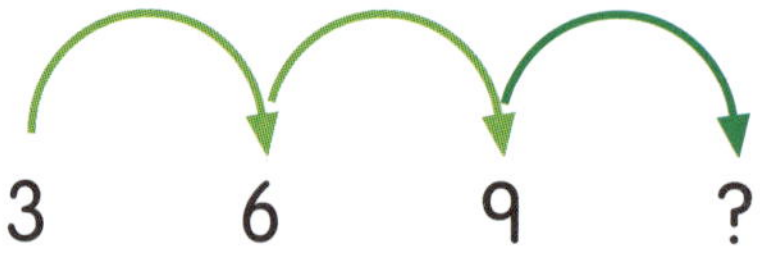

She has 12 pears altogether.

3 Jack has 8 pieces of paper.
There are 3 stickers on each piece of paper.
How many stickers does Jack have altogether?

___ × ___ = ___

Jack has ___ stickers altogether.

Activity

4

Crack the code on the wheel.

Find out what Millie got for her birthday.

Copy and complete the multiplication sentences.

R 4 × 3 = ☐	**O** 7 × 3 = ☐
L 2 × 3 = ☐	**E** 8 × 3 = ☐
M 9 × 3 = ☐	**P** 5 × 3 = ☐
A 6 × 3 = ☐	**I** 3 × 3 = ☐
N 10 × 3 = ☐	**T** 1 × 3 = ☐

Match the letters to the answers.

☐	☐	☐	☐	☐	☐	☐	☐	☐	☐	☐
18	3	12	18	27	15	21	6	9	30	24

Practice Book 2B, p.11

Let's Learn!

Multiplying by 3: using dot paper

1 There are 4 hens.
Each hen lays 3 eggs.
How many eggs do they lay altogether?

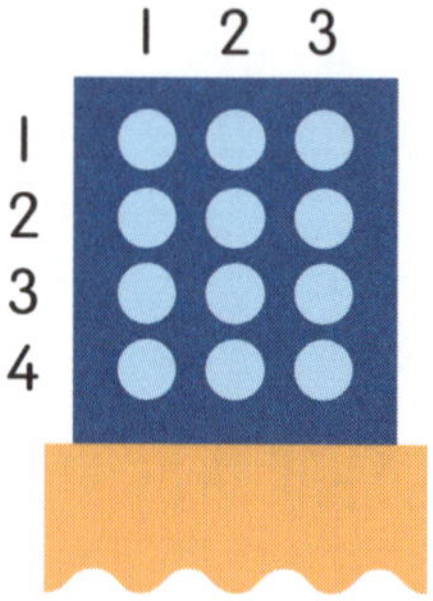

$4 \times 3 = 12$

They lay 12 eggs altogether.

2 Hardeep has 6 boxes of crayons.
Each box contains 3 crayons.
How many crayons are there altogether?

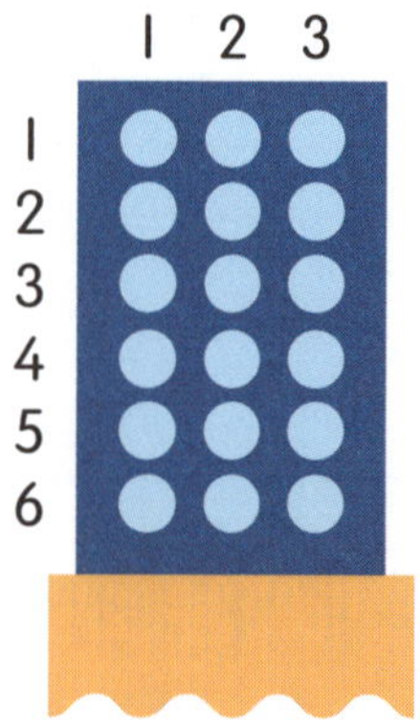

$6 \times 3 =$ ____

There are ____ crayons altogether.

3 Ruby packs 3 apples into 1 bag.
How many apples are there in 5 bags?

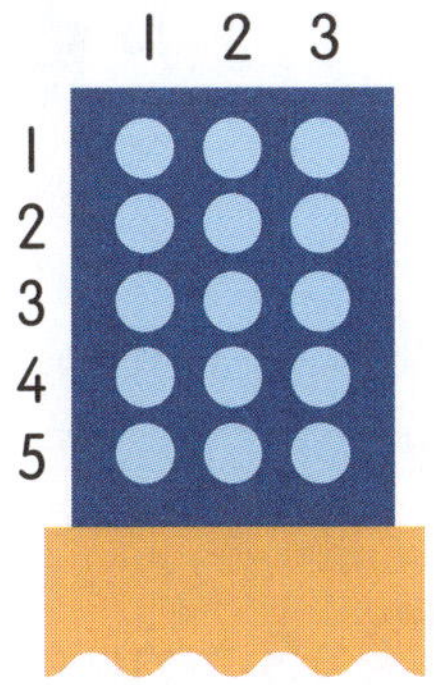

5 × 3 = ☐

There are ☐ apples in 5 bags.

4 Short cuts!

a 6 × 3 = ?
Start with 5 groups of 3.

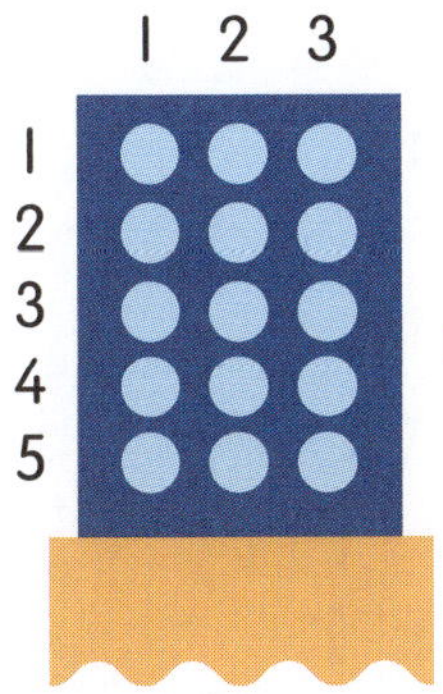

5 × 3 = 15

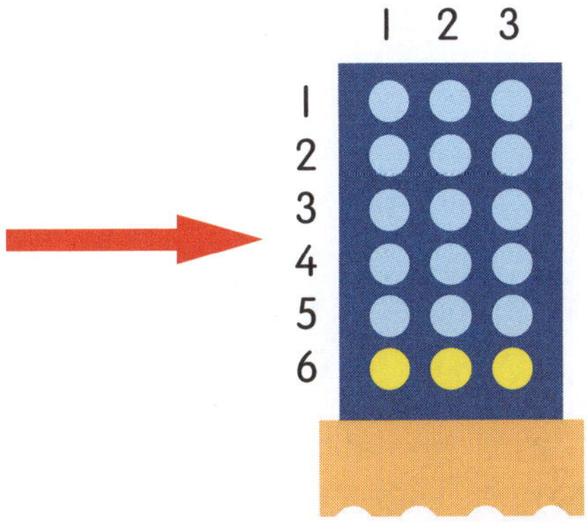

6 × 3 = 15 + 3
= 18

b $8 \times 3 = ?$

Start with 10 groups of 3.

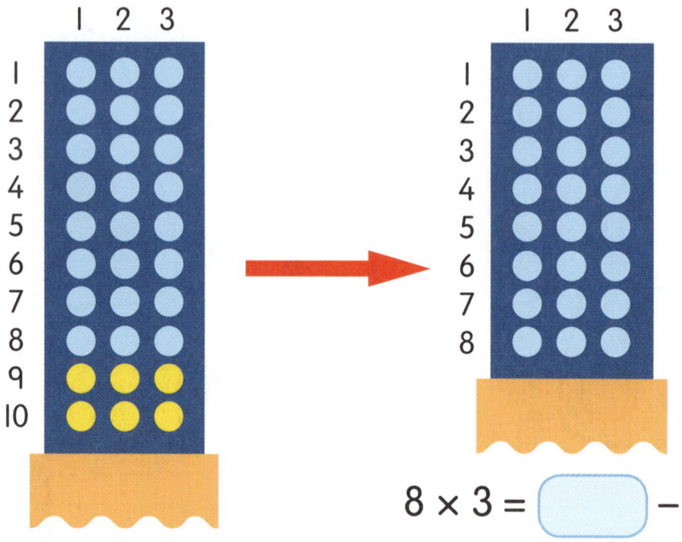

$10 \times 3 =$ ☐

$8 \times 3 =$ ☐ $- 6$

$=$ ☐

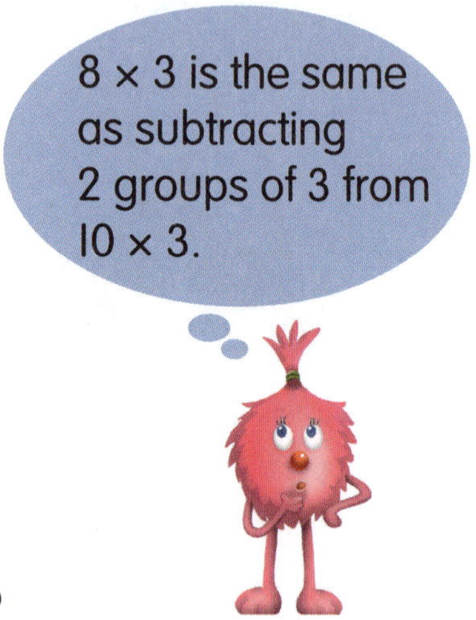

5 3 times table

1	×	3	=	3
2	×	3	=	6
3	×	3	=	9
4	×	3	=	12
5	×	3	=	15
6	×	3	=	18
7	×	3	=	21
8	×	3	=	24
9	×	3	=	27
10	×	3	=	30

6 $4 \times 3 = 12$

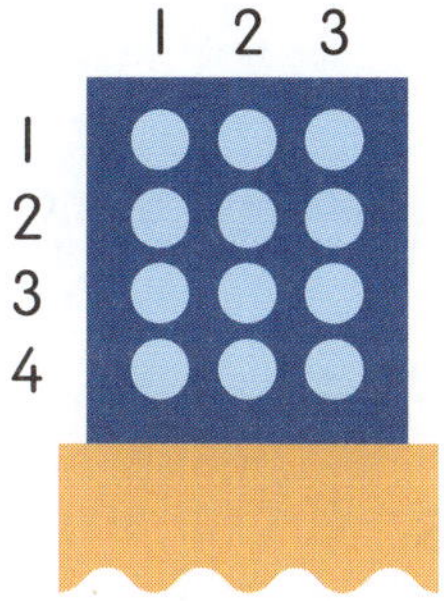

$3 \times 4 = 12$

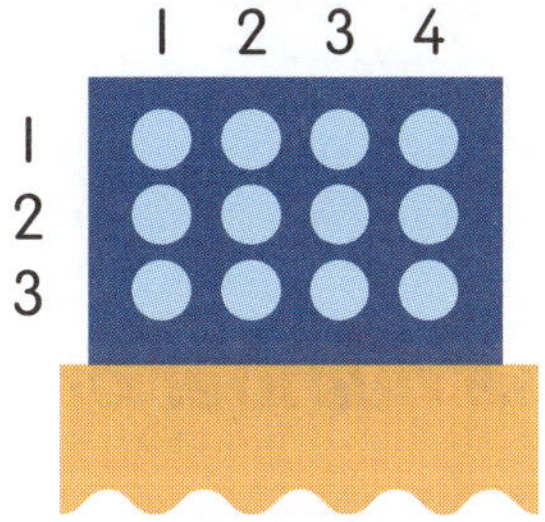

7 Find the missing numbers.
Use the dot paper to help you.

$\square \times \square = 21$ $\qquad$ $\square \times \square = 21$

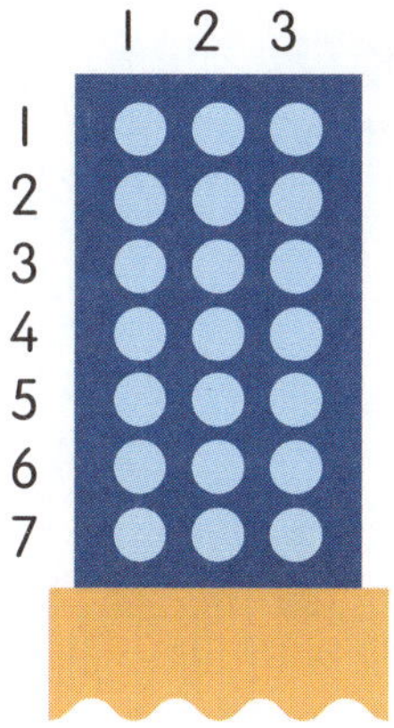

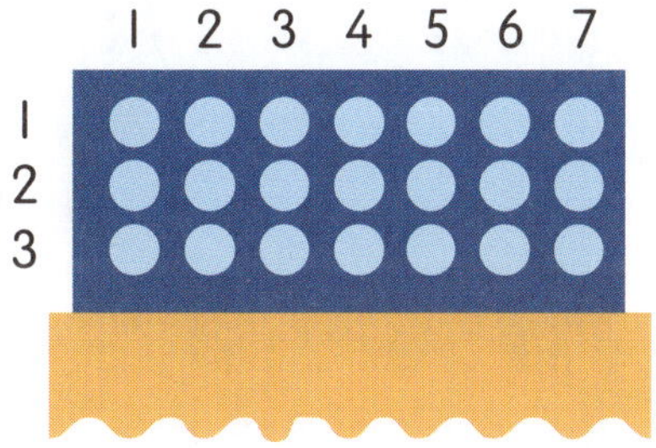

8 Answer these questions.

a $5 \times 3 = \square$ $\qquad$ $7 \times 3 = \square + 6 = \square$

b $10 \times 3 = \square$ $\qquad$ $9 \times 3 = \square - 3 = \square$

c $6 \times 3 = \square$ $\qquad$ $3 \times 6 = \square$

d $8 \times 3 = \square$ $\qquad$ $3 \times 8 = \square$

Practice Book 2B, p.13

Let's Learn!

Division

Sharing: Finding the number of items in each group

1 Divide 12 pencil sharpeners into 2 equal groups.
How many pencil sharpeners are there in each group?

$12 \div 2 = ?$

$2 \times 6 = 12$
$12 \div 2 = 6$

There are 6 pencil sharpeners in each group.

2 Divide 12 spoons into 3 equal groups.
How many spoons are there in each group?

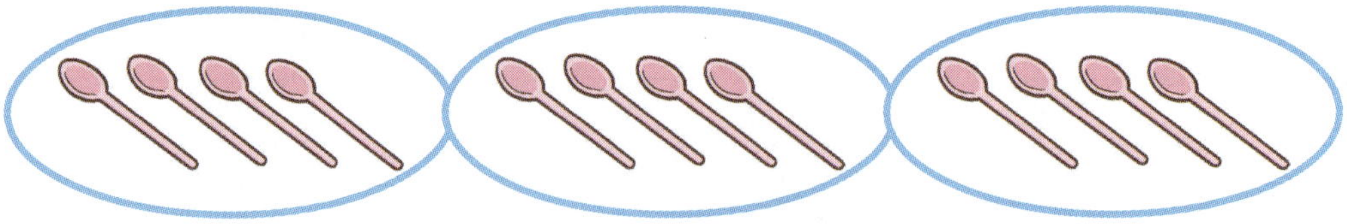

$12 \div 3 = ?$

$3 \times \square = 12$
$12 \div 3 = \square$

There are $\square$ spoons in each group.

3 2 children share 8 crackers equally between themselves.
How many crackers does each child get?

$8 \div 2 = \square$

Each child gets $\square$ crackers.

4 Peter divides 6 balls equally into 3 tubes.
How many balls are there in each tube?

$6 \div 3 = \square$

There are $\square$ balls in each tube.

Grouping: Making Equal Groups

5 Divide 15 jelly beans into equal groups.
There are 3 jelly beans in each group.
How many groups are there?

$15 \div 3 = ?$

There are 5 groups.

6 Divide 16 marbles into equal groups.
There are 2 marbles in each group.
How many groups are there?

$16 \div 2 = ?$

There are 8 groups.

7 Divide 18 buttons into equal groups.
There are 3 buttons in each group.
How many groups are there?

$18 \div 3 = ?$

There are ☐ groups.

8 Hardeep has 20 carrots.
He divides them equally onto plates.
There are 2 carrots on each plate.
How many plates of carrots are there?

$20 \div 2 = ?$

There are ☐ plates of carrots.

9 Answer these questions.

a Ruby puts 14 buttons equally into 2 plastic bags.
How many buttons are there in each plastic bag?

b Millie and Ella have 24 coloured pencils altogether.
They tie the pencils into bundles of 3.
How many bundles are there?

Practice Book 2B, p.17

Let's Explore!

10 Jack has fewer than 8 straws.
He decides to put them into groups.

This is what he finds:

a When he puts 2 straws in each group, there are no straws left.

b When he puts 3 straws in each group, there are no straws left.

How many straws does Jack have?

Put On Your Thinking Caps!

11 Find the missing number.

Practice Book 2B, p.21
Practice Book 2B, p.22

Unit 6 Multiplying by 4, 5 and 10

Let's Learn!

Multiplying by 4: skip-counting

1 There are 4 clothes pegs in 1 group.

$2 \times 4 = 8$

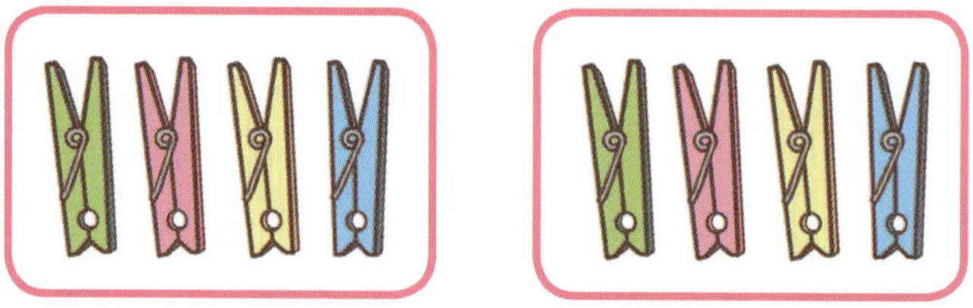

How many clothes pegs are there in 10 groups?

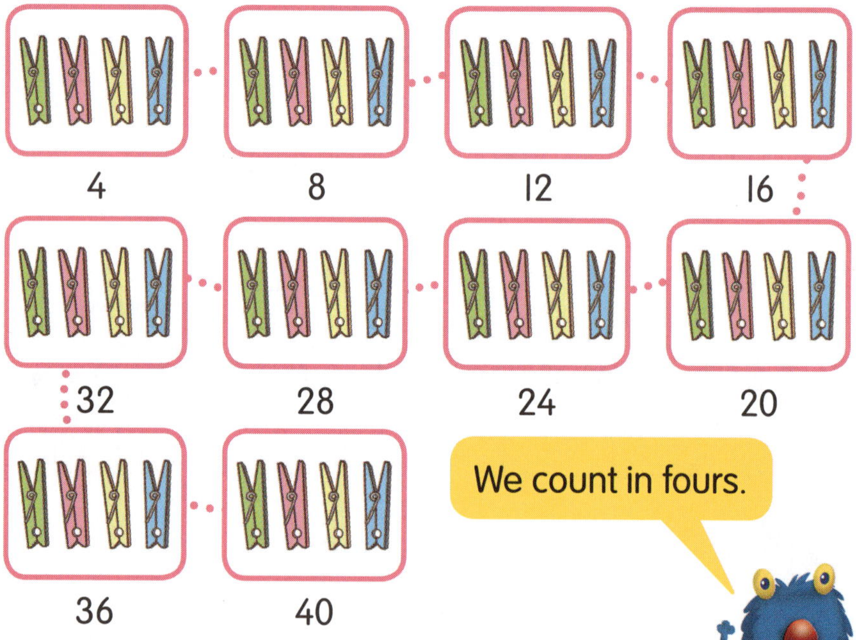

4, 8, 12, 16, 20, 24, 28, 32, 36, 40

$10 \times 4 = 40$

There are 40 clothes pegs in 10 groups.

2 Jack has 7 bags.
There are 4 marbles in each bag.
How many marbles does Jack have altogether?

7 groups of 4 marbles

7 × 4 = ?

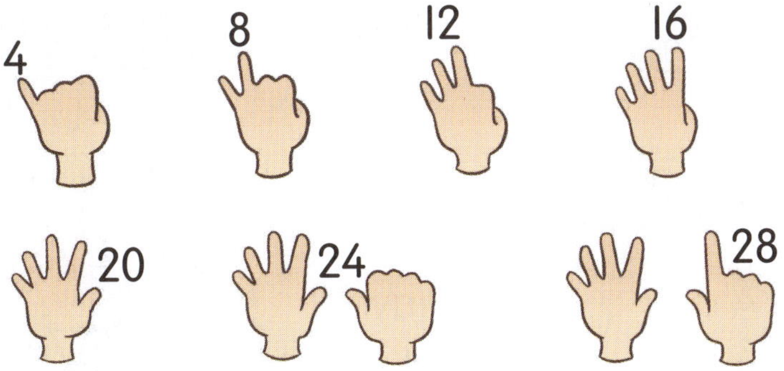

We count in fours.
4, 8, 12, 16,
20, 24, 28

Jack has 28 marbles altogether.

3 There are 3 frogs in a pond.
Each frog has 4 legs.
How many legs do the frogs have altogether?

3 groups of 4 legs

We count in fours.
4, ☐, ☐

☐ × ☐ = ☐

The frogs have ☐ legs altogether.

Game

Players: 3 to 4

You will need:
- cut-outs of a rocket
- stickers or masking tape
- two dice

4 Two-dice game

How to play:

1 Stick these numbers on the dice as shown.

Dice A:

2/3 4/5 6/7 6/8 8/9 7/9

Dice B:

2 3 4 2 3 4

2 Each player has a cut-out rocket.

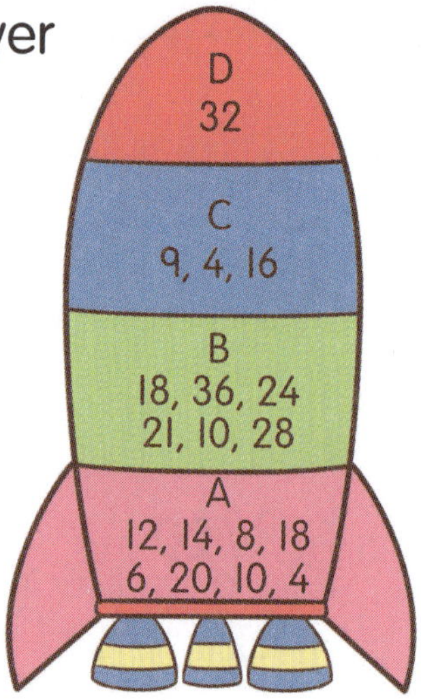

3 Player 1 rolls Dice A and chooses one of the two numbers.

4 Player 1 rolls Dice B for the next number and multiplies the two numbers.

5 Player 1 shades out the answer on the rocket. The other players check the answer.

6 Take turns. Players must shade out all of Stage A before moving to the next stage.

The first person to complete all four stages on their rocket wins!

Practice Book 2B, p.23

Let's Learn!

Multiplying by 4: using dot paper

1

Ruby has 5 toy cars.

Each car has 4 wheels.

How many wheels are there altogether?

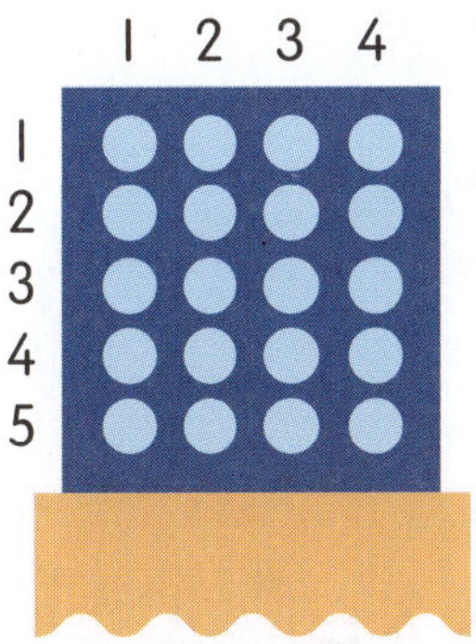

There are 20 wheels altogether.

2 Jack has 9 pictures.
He puts sticky tape on each corner of the pictures.
How many pieces of sticky tape does Jack use altogether?

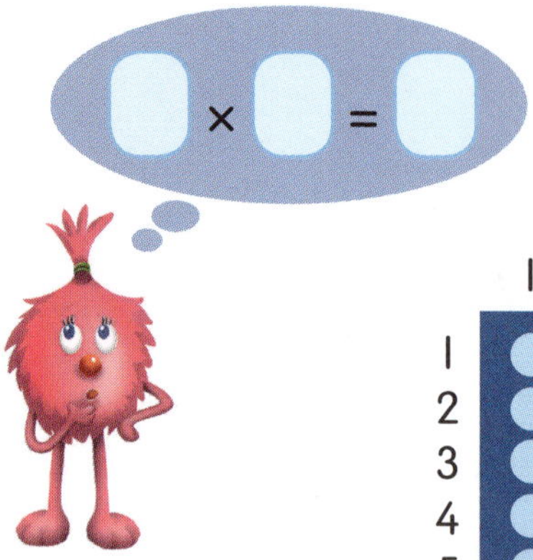

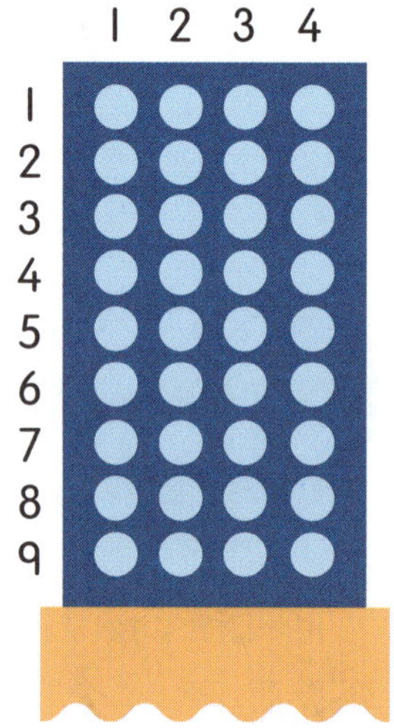

Jack uses ☐ pieces of sticky tape altogether.

3 Answer these questions.
Use dot paper to help you multiply.

Example

3 × 4 = 12

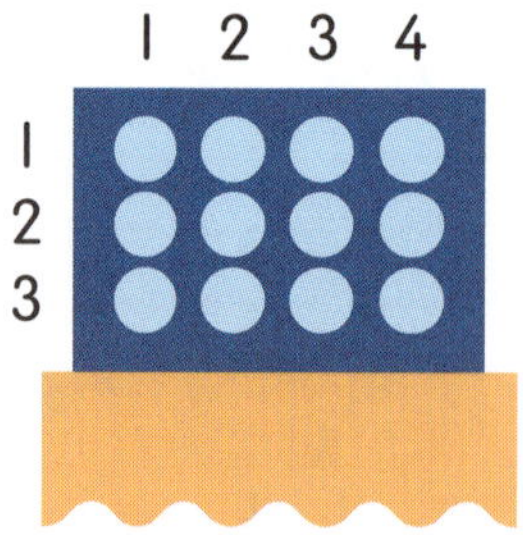

a 4 × 4 = ☐ **b** 6 × 4 = ☐

c 7 × 4 = ☐ **d** 8 × 4 = ☐

Activity

4

Crack the code on the wheel.

Find out what Millie had for breakfast.

Copy and complete each multiplication sentence.

R	$6 \times 4 =$ ☐	**C**	$5 \times 4 =$ ☐
O	$3 \times 4 =$ ☐	**L**	$8 \times 4 =$ ☐
S	$9 \times 4 =$ ☐	**N**	$10 \times 4 =$ ☐
F	$4 \times 4 =$ ☐	**E**	$1 \times 4 =$ ☐
A	$2 \times 4 =$ ☐	**K**	$7 \times 4 =$ ☐

Match the letters to the answers.

☐	☐	☐	☐		☐	☐	☐	☐	☐	☐
20	12	24	40		16	32	8	28	4	36

5 Short cuts!

a $6 \times 4 = ?$

Start with 5 groups of 4.

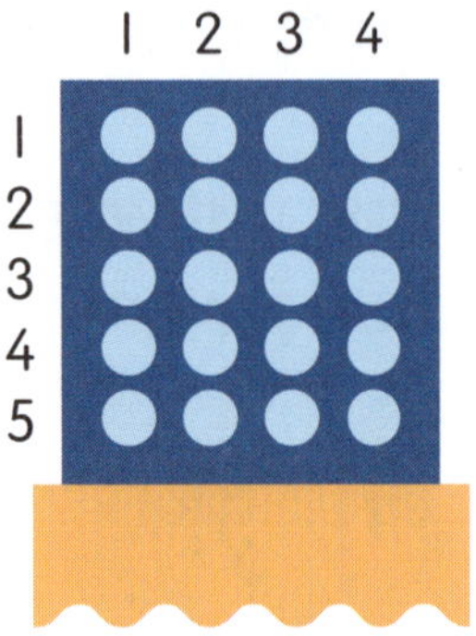

$5 \times 4 = 20$

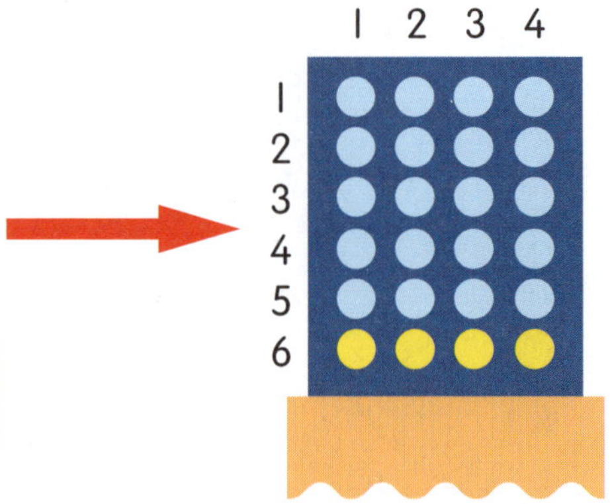

$6 \times 4 = 20 + 4$

$= 24$

b $9 \times 4 = ?$

Start with 10 groups of 4.

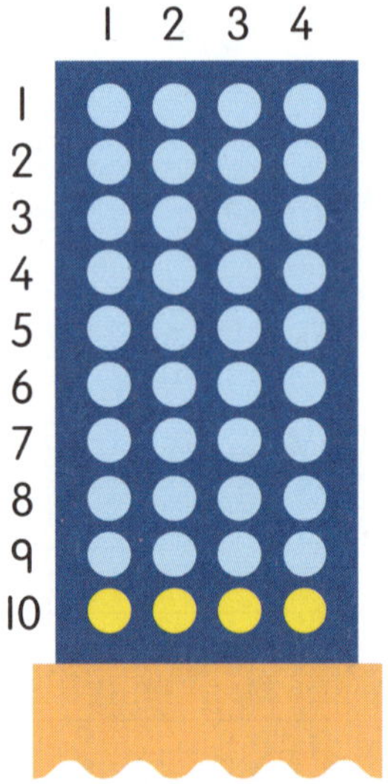

$10 \times 4 = 40$

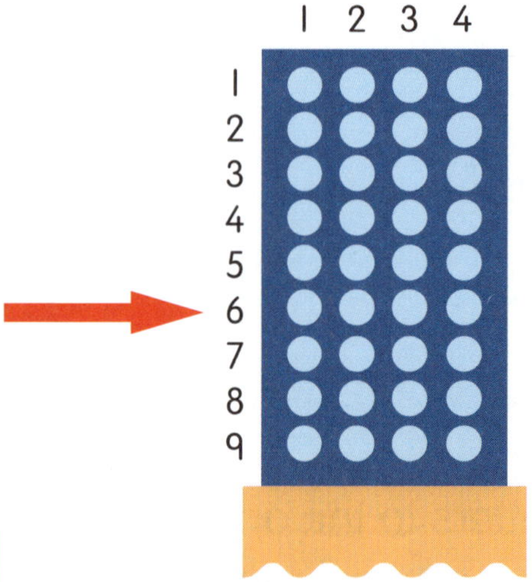

$9 \times 4 = 40 - 4$

$= 36$

c $8 \times 4 = ?$

Start with 10 groups of 4.

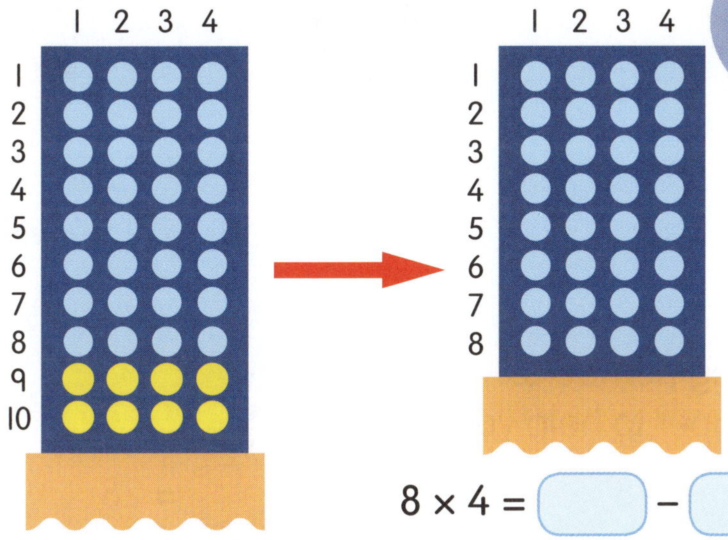

$10 \times 4 =$ ☐

$8 \times 4 =$ ☐ $-$ ☐

$=$ ☐

8 × 4 is the same as subtracting 2 groups of 4 from 10 × 4.

6 4 times table

1	×	4	=	4
2	×	4	=	8
3	×	4	=	12
4	×	4	=	16
5	×	4	=	20
6	×	4	=	24
7	×	4	=	28
8	×	4	=	32
9	×	4	=	36
10	×	4	=	40

7 $2 \times 4 = 8$

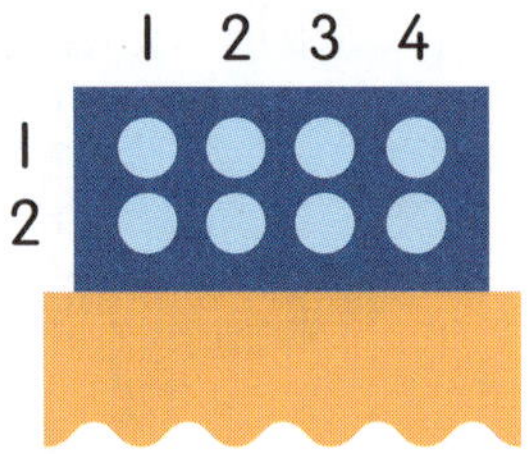

$4 \times 2 = 8$

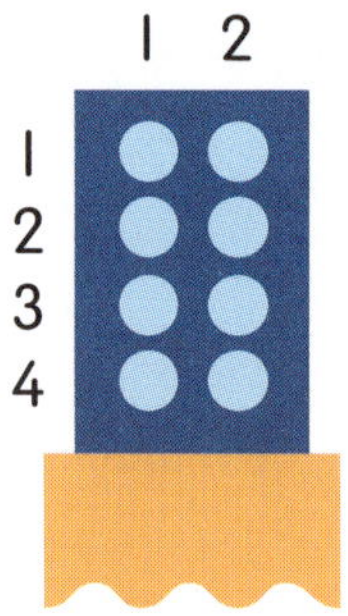

8 Find the missing numbers.
Use the dot paper to help you.

☐ × ☐ = 28

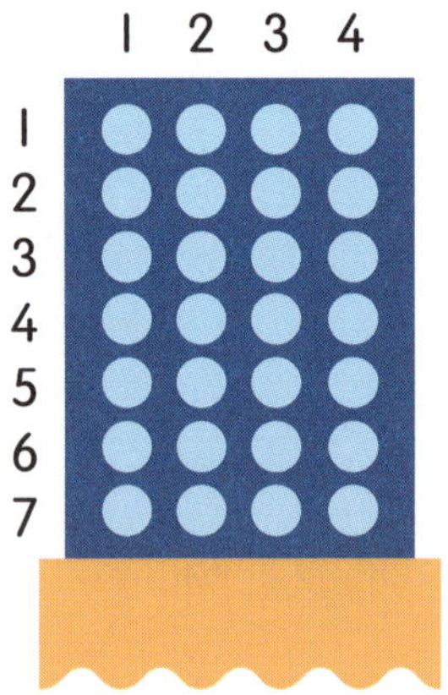

☐ × ☐ = 28

9 Answer these questions.

a $5 \times 4 =$ ☐ $7 \times 4 =$ ☐ $+ 8 =$ ☐

b $10 \times 4 =$ ☐ $9 \times 4 =$ ☐ $- 4 =$ ☐

c $3 \times 4 =$ ☐ $4 \times 3 =$ ☐

d $8 \times 4 =$ ☐ $4 \times 8 =$ ☐

Practice Book 2B, p.25

Let's Learn!

Multiplying by 5: skip-counting

1 I finger stands for I group of 5.
I × 5 = 5

What do 10 fingers stand for?

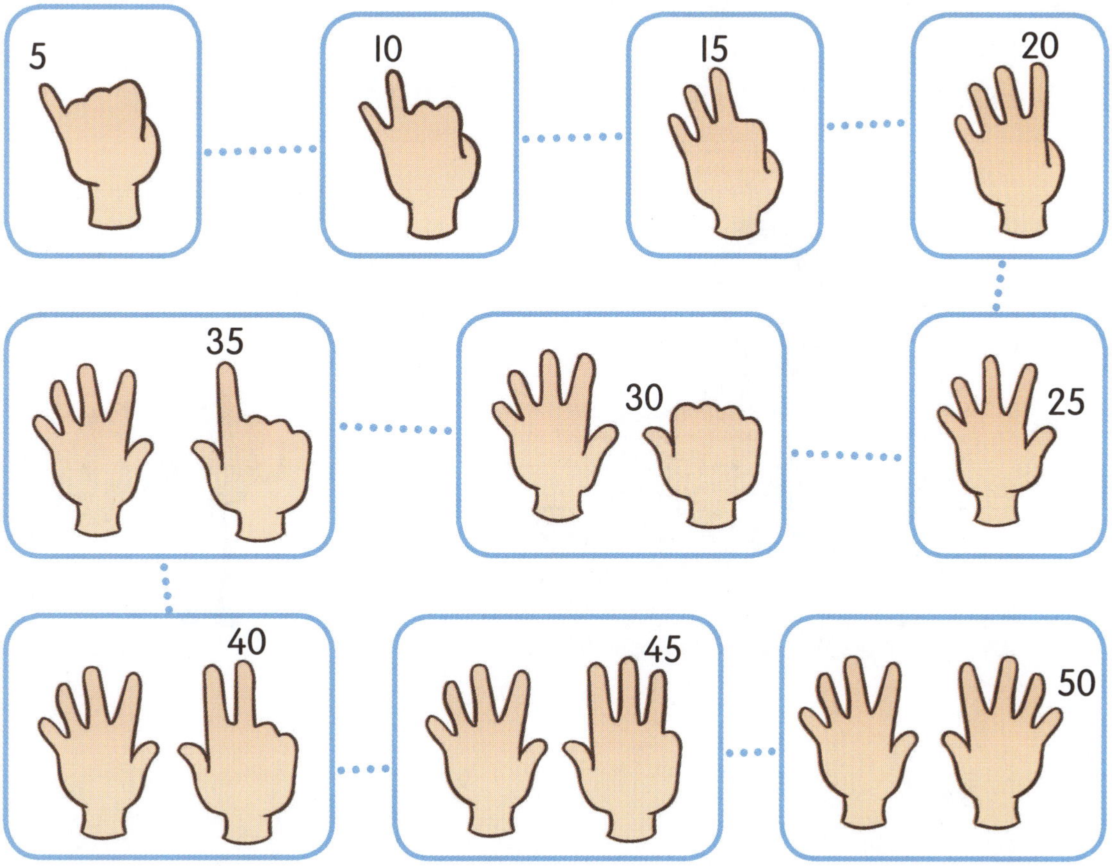

10 × 5 = 50

10 fingers stand for 50.

2 Ella has 7 bunches of flowers.
Each bunch has 5 flowers.
How many flowers does she have altogether?

$7 \times 5 = ?$

7 groups of 5 flowers

We count in fives. 5, 10, 15, 20, 25, 30, 35

Ella has 35 flowers altogether.

3 Farha has 6 starfish in her tank.
Each starfish has 5 arms.
How many arms do the 6 starfish have altogether?

We count in fives.
5, 10, ___, ___, ___, ___

6 groups of 5 arms

___ × ___ = ___

They have ___ arms altogether.

Game

Players: 3 to 4

You will need:

- a chart
- a 10-sided dice
- a counter labelled 4 and 5

4 Roll and multiply

How to play:

1 Each player will need a chart to record their answers.

×	1	2	3	4	5	6	7	8	9	10
4										
5										

2 Player 1 throws the dice and tosses the counter.

3 Player 1 multiplies the two numbers.

4 Player 1 writes the answer in their chart. The others check the answer.
Take turns to play.

The first person to complete the chart wins!

Practice Book 2B, p.29

Let's Learn!

Multiplying by 5: using dot paper

1 Tai has 3 vases.
He puts 5 flowers into each vase.
How many flowers are there altogether?

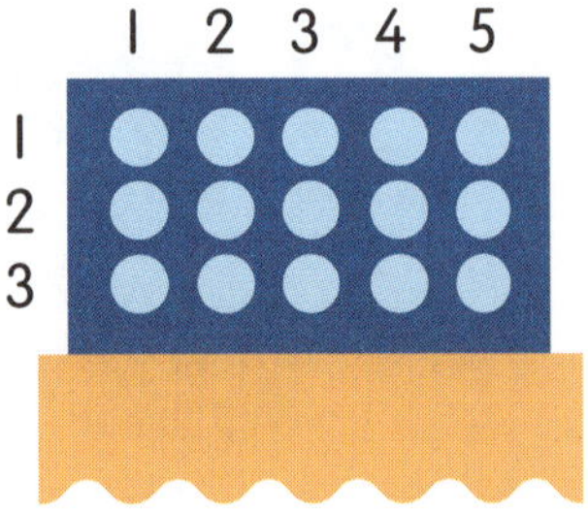

There are 15 flowers altogether.

2 Ella has 2 fish tanks.
Each tank has 5 goldfish.
How many goldfish are there altogether?

There are ____ goldfish altogether.

Activity

3 **a** Look at the picture.
Use multiplication sentences to tell your friends a story about the birds and nests.

Make up a question to find the number of birds.

b Make up your own multiplication story!
Ask your friends to find the number of things in your story.

4 Short cuts!

a $3 \times 5 = ?$

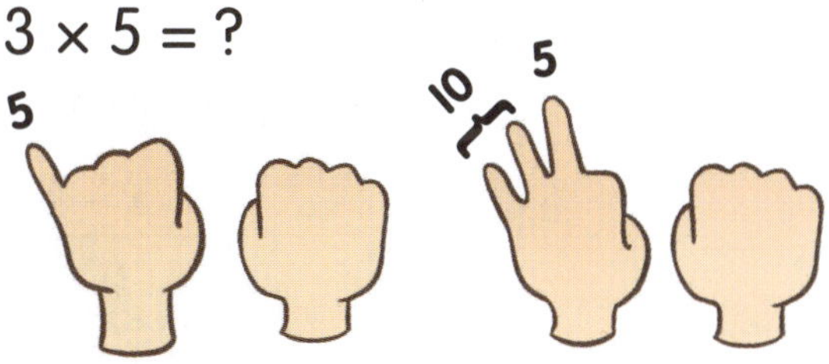

One finger stands for 5.
Two fingers stand for 10.
Three fingers stand for $10 + 5 = 15$.

$$3 \times 5 = 10 + 5$$
$$= 15$$

b $7 \times 5 = ?$

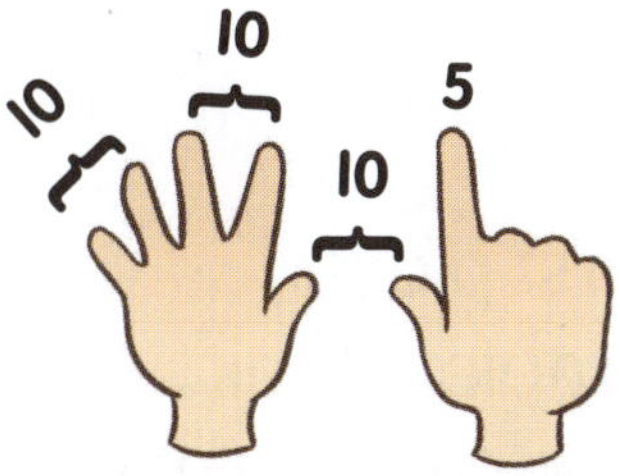

10, 20, 30, 35
$7 \times 5 = 35$

$$7 \times 5 = 10 + 10 + 10 + 5$$
$$= 35$$

c $4 \times 5 = ?$

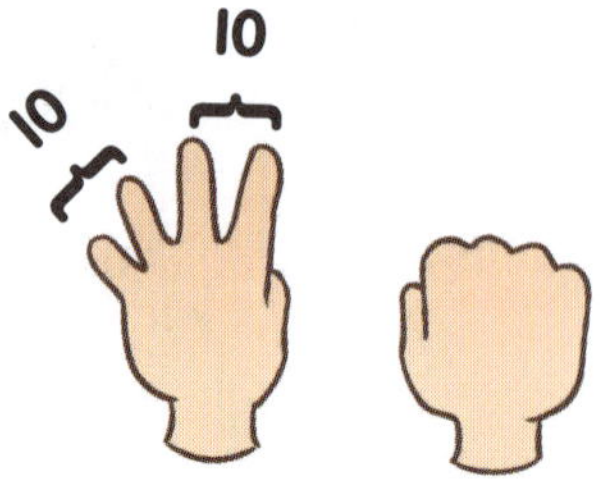

$4 \times 5 =$ ☐

Activity

Players: 3 to 4

You will need:

- a spinner sheet
- a spinner

5 Spin and multiply!

How to play:

1 Each player is given a spinner sheet.

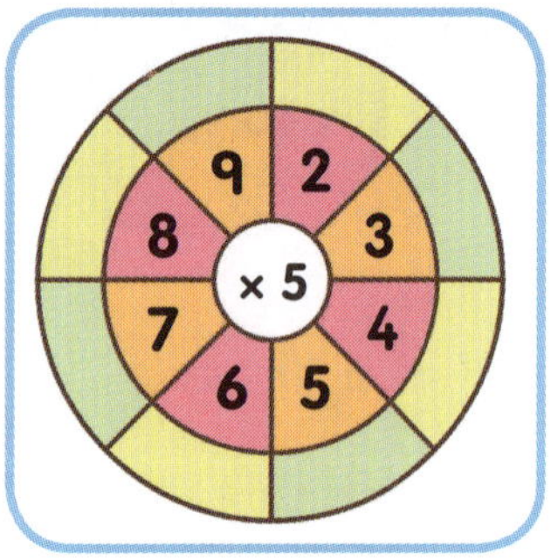

2 Player 1 spins the spinner.

3 Player 1 multiplies this number by 5. They fill in the answer on their spinner sheet.

4 The other players check the answer. Take turns to play.

The first player to complete their spinner sheet wins!

6 5 times table

1	×	5	=	5
2	×	5	=	10
3	×	5	=	15
4	×	5	=	20
5	×	5	=	25
6	×	5	=	30
7	×	5	=	35
8	×	5	=	40
9	×	5	=	45
10	×	5	=	50

7 $2 \times 5 = 10$

$5 \times 2 = 10$

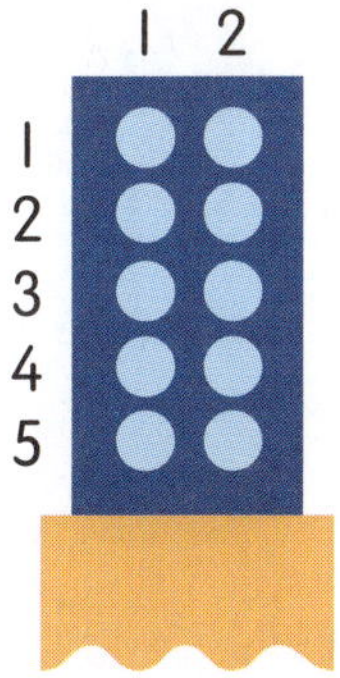

8 Find the missing numbers.
Use the dot paper to help you.

$\square \times \square = 20$

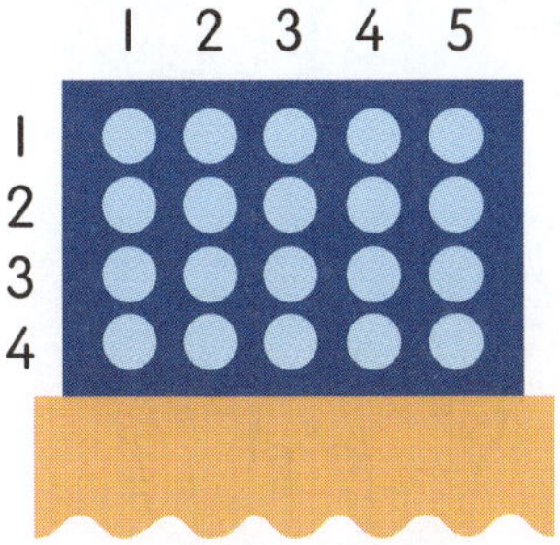

$\square \times \square = 20$

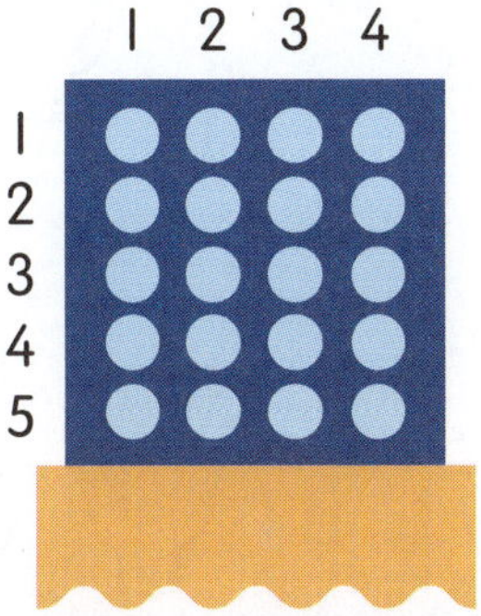

Practice Book 2B, p.33

Let's Learn!

Multiplying by 10: skip-counting and using dot paper

1

I group of 10 sticks.

$1 \times 10 = 10$

2

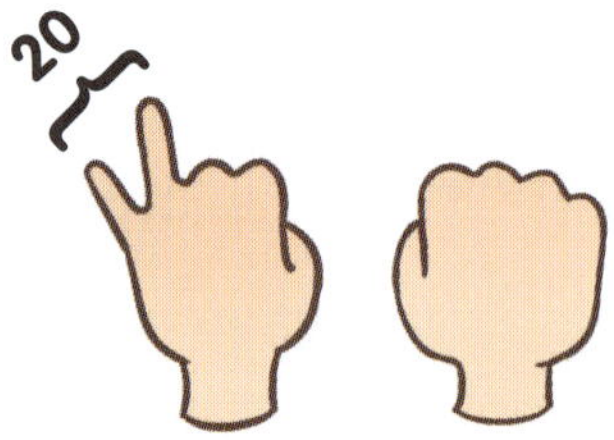

2 groups of 10 sticks.

$2 \times 10 = 20$

Count in tens with your fingers.

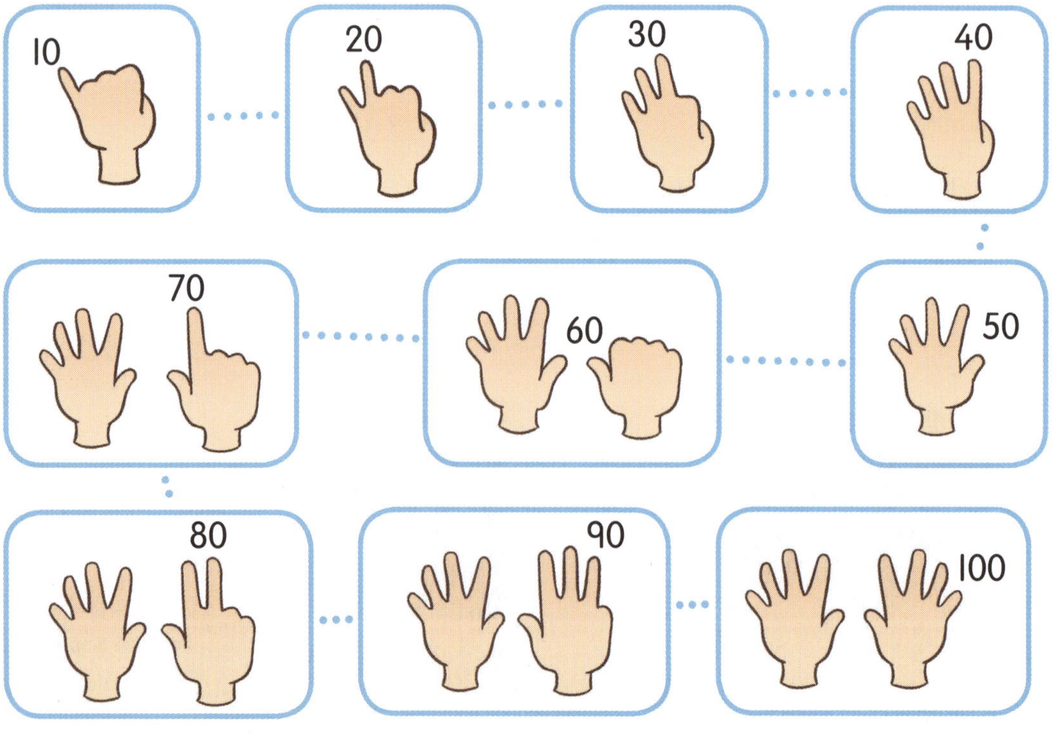

3 Omar has 6 lorries.
Each lorry has 10 wheels.

How many wheels are there on the lorries altogether?

6 groups of 10 wheels

I count in tens.
10, 20, ☐, ☐, ☐, ☐

☐ × ☐ = ☐

There are ☐ wheels on the lorries altogether.

Activity

4 **a** Look at the picture.
Use multiplication sentences to tell your friends a story about the trays and the bags of popcorn.

Make a question to find the number of bags of popcorn.

b Look at the picture.
Use multiplication sentences to tell your friends a story about the tiles and footprints.
Make a question to find the number of footprints.

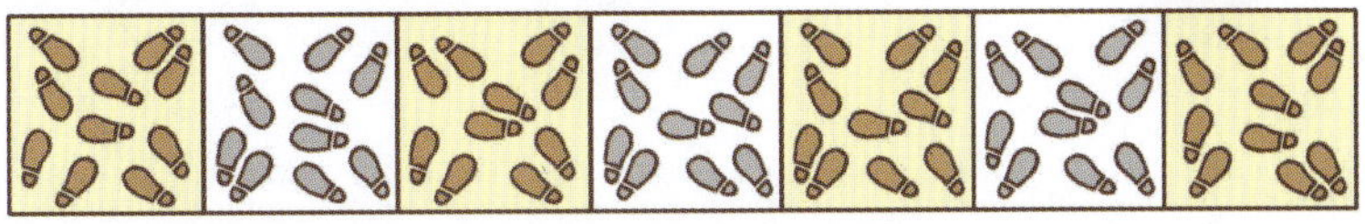

5 Short cuts!

I have a shorter way to multiply.
3 × 1 = 3
3 × 10 = 30

Find the missing numbers.

1 × 1 = ☐, 1 × 10 = ☐

2 × 1 = ☐, 2 × 10 = ☐

3 × 1 = ☐, 3 × 10 = ☐

4 × 1 = ☐, 4 × 10 = ☐

5 × 1 = ☐, 5 × 10 = ☐

What pattern do you see in the answers?

6 Answer these questions.

a 6 × 10 = ☐ **b** 7 × 10 = ☐ **c** 9 × 10 = ☐

7 10 times table

1	×	10	=	10
2	×	10	=	20
3	×	10	=	30
4	×	10	=	40
5	×	10	=	50
6	×	10	=	60
7	×	10	=	70
8	×	10	=	80
9	×	10	=	90
10	×	10	=	100

8 $3 \times 10 = 30$

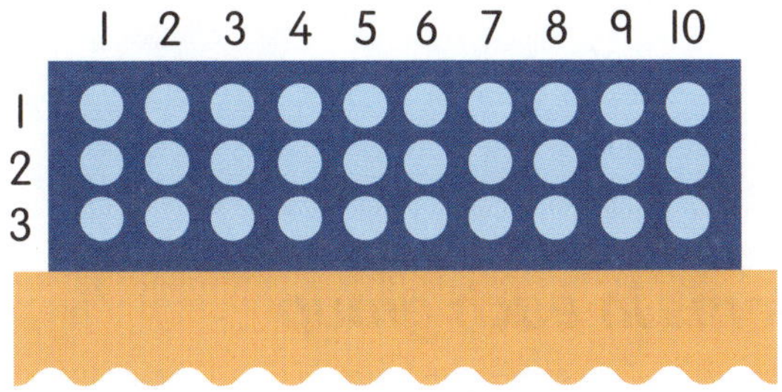

$10 \times 3 = 30$

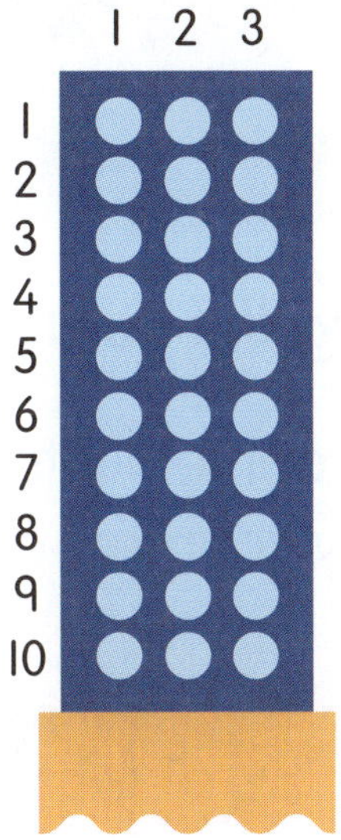

9 Find the missing numbers.
Use the dot paper to help you.

☐ × ☐ = 80 ☐ × ☐ = 80

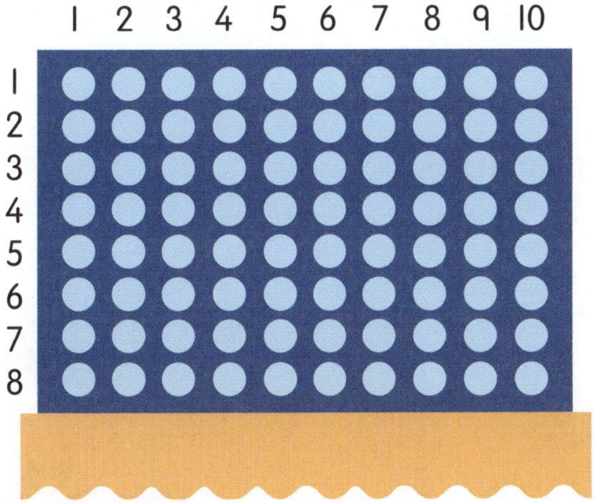

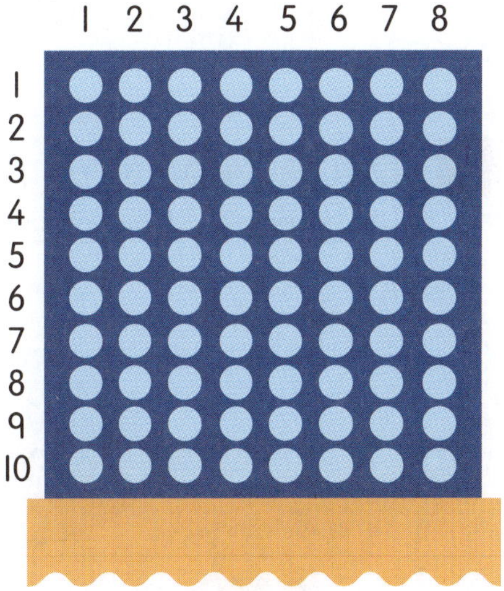

10 Answer these questions.

a $6 \times 10 =$ ☐ $10 \times 6 =$ ☐

b $9 \times 10 =$ ☐ $10 \times 9 =$ ☐

Practice Book 2B, p.35

Let's Learn!

Division

Sharing: finding the number of items in each group

1 Divide 15 counters into 5 equal groups.
How many counters are there in each group?

$15 \div 5 = ?$

$5 \times 3 = 15$
$15 \div 5 = 3$

There are 3 counters in each group.

2 Divide 24 buttons into 4 equal groups.
How many buttons are there in each group?

$24 \div 4 = ?$

$4 \times \square = 24$
$24 \div 4 = \square$

There are $\square$ buttons in each group.

3 4 friends share 28 blueberries equally.
How many blueberries does each friend get?

$28 \div \square = \square$

Each friend gets ☐ blueberries.

4 Put 40 shells equally into 10 trays.
How many shells are there in each tray?

$40 \div 10 = \square$

There are ☐ shells in each tray.

Activity

5 Tell a division story.

Ask your friends to act out your story by using counters.
Then use the counters to find the answer to the division story.
Take turns to tell stories!

Grouping: making equal groups

6 Divide 35 blocks into equal groups.
There are 5 blocks in each group.
How many groups are there?

$35 \div 5 = ?$

$7 \times 5 = 35$
$35 \div 5 = 7$

There are 7 groups.

7 Divide 30 paper stars into equal groups.
There are 5 paper stars in each group.
How many groups are there?

$30 \div 5 = ?$

$\square \times 5 = 30$
$30 \div 5 = \square$.

There are $\square$ groups.

8 Divide 36 beads into equal groups.
There are 4 beads in each group.
How many groups are there?

36 ÷ 4 = ☐

There are ☐ groups.

Game

Players: 3 to 4

You will need:

- ten multiplication cards of 2, 4, 5 and 10

9 **Number game!**

How to play:

1 Shuffle the multiplication cards. Player 1 takes a card.

Example

If a card **2 × 4 = 8** is taken, the rest of the group write **8 ÷ 2 = 4** or **8 ÷ 4 = 2**.

2 The other players write one division sentence for the card.

3 Player 1 checks their answers.

4 Take turns to take a card. Play four rounds.

The player with the most correct answers wins!

10 Look at each multiplication sentence.
Then find the missing numbers for the division sentences.

a $2 \times 4 = 8$ $8 \div 2 = 4$
$8 \div 4 = 2$

b $3 \times 10 = 30$ $30 \div 3 = \square$
$30 \div \square = \square$

11 Find the missing numbers.
Then write two division sentences for each of them.

a $\square \times 5 = 40$ **b** $\square \times 4 = 28$

12 Answer these questions.

a Ella puts 20 skipping ropes equally into 5 boxes.
How many skipping ropes are there in each box?

b Miya buys a box of 80 beads.
She uses 10 beads to make a bracelet.
How many bracelets could she make with the whole box of beads?

Practice Book 2B, p.39

Put On Your Thinking Caps!

13 Omar reads a book.
He reads the same number of pages each day.
He stops at page 12 after 3 days.
How many pages does he read each day?

Use the diagram to help you answer the question.

Practice Book 2B, p.43
Practice Book 2B, p.44

Unit 7 Using Models: Multiplication and Division

Let's Learn!

Multiplication

1 Peter puts 5 bread rolls into each packet.
He has 4 packets.
How many bread rolls does he put into the 4 packets altogether?

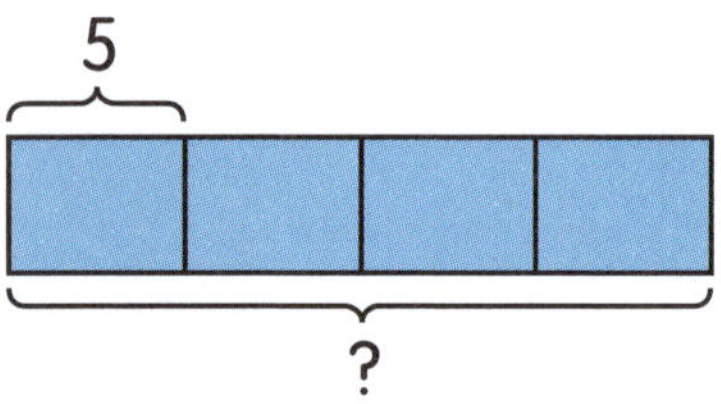

$4 \times 5 = 20$

Peter puts 20 bread rolls into the 4 packets.

2 Jack counts 3 nests in a tree.
There are 6 birds in each nest.
How many birds are there altogether?

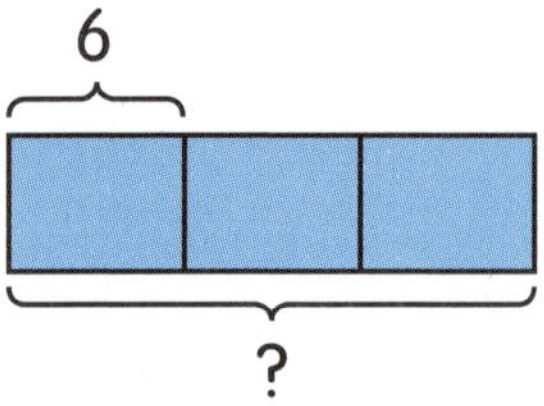

___ × ___ = ___

There are ___ birds altogether.

Activity

3 Work in pairs.
You will need some coloured strips.
Use the strips to make models.
Then solve the word problems.

Example

Millie has 4 plates.
There are 3 pieces of fruit on each plate.
How many pieces of fruit are there altogether?

1 Choose 4 coloured strips of the same length to show 4 plates. Stick them on a piece of paper to make a model.

2 Write the numbers and words of the word problem on the model. Write the number 3 above one of the strips to show 3 fruits each.

3 Complete the model. Then find the answer.

4 Write the multiplication sentence: $4 \times 3 = 12$

a Mrs Green and Mrs Lee bought 8 pizzas each.
How many pizzas did they buy altogether?

b A baker uses 10 eggs to make a cake.
He makes 4 cakes.
How many eggs does he use altogether?

Practice Book 2B, p.49

Let's Learn!

Division

1 Hardeep buys 12 pears.
He puts an equal number of pears into 3 boxes.
How many pears are there in each box?

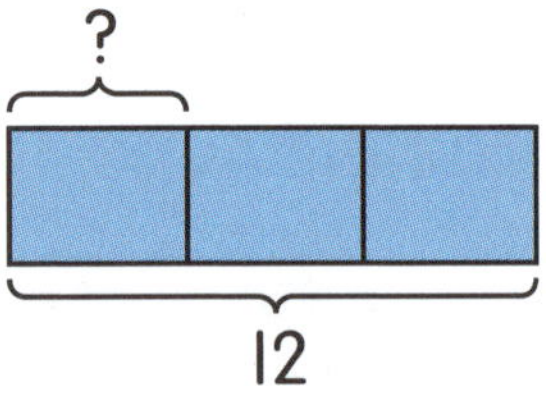

$12 \div 3 = 4$

There are 4 pears in each box.

2 Peter makes 5 shapes with 30 straws.
He uses the same number of straws for each shape.
How many straws does Peter use to make each shape?

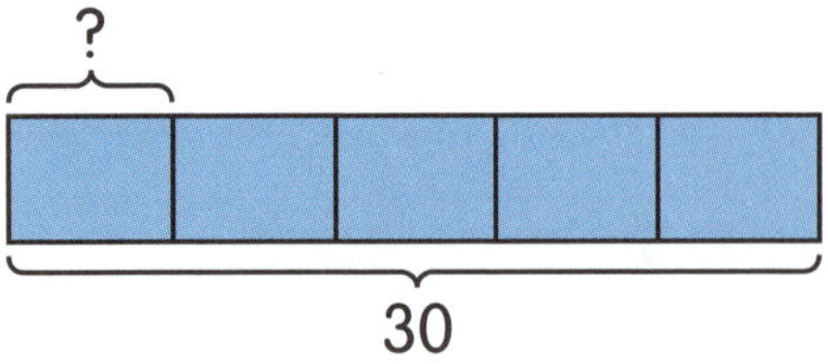

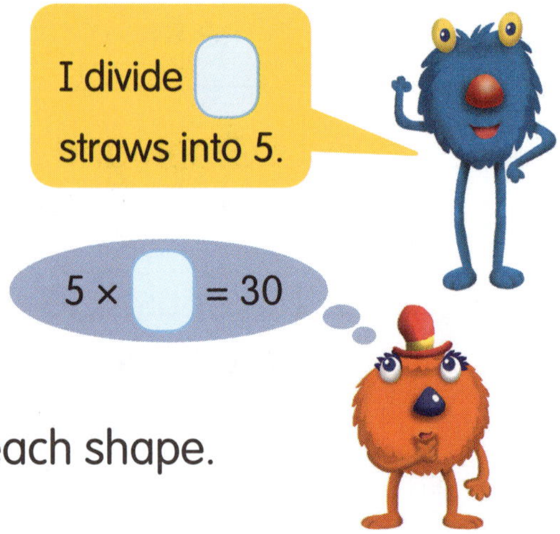

$30 \div 5 =$ ____

Peter uses ____ straws to make each shape.

Activity

3 Work in pairs.
You will need some coloured strips.
Use the strips to make models.
Then solve the word problems.

Example

Miss Lee has 15 cards.
She gives out these cards equally to 5 children.
How many cards does each child get?

1 Choose 5 coloured strips of the same length to show 5 children. Stick them on a piece of paper to make a model.

2 Write the number 15 below the model. Complete the model. Then find the answer.

3 Write the division sentence: $15 \div 5 = 3$

a Farha has 18 stamps and 3 envelopes.
She puts the same number of stamps on each envelope.
How many stamps does she put on each envelope?

b Omar saves £20 in 4 days.
He saves an equal amount each day.
How much does Omar save each day?

4 Miya makes 15 cakes.
She puts the cakes into boxes.
There are 3 cakes in each box.
How many boxes does Miya use altogether?

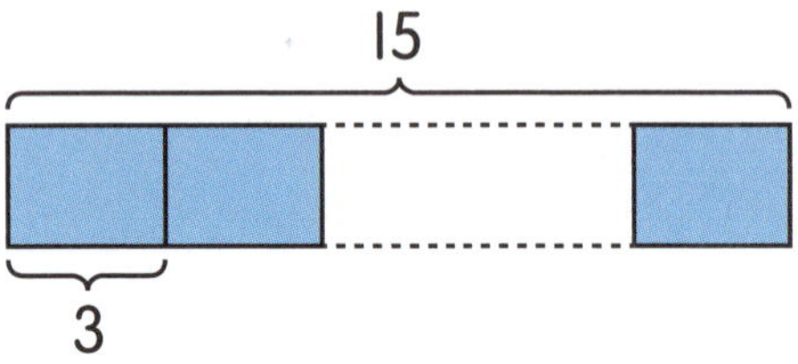

$15 \div 3 = 5$

Miya uses 5 boxes altogether.

5 Sally has 20 pieces of wood for making picture frames.
She uses 4 pieces of wood for each picture frame.
How many picture frames does Sally make altogether?

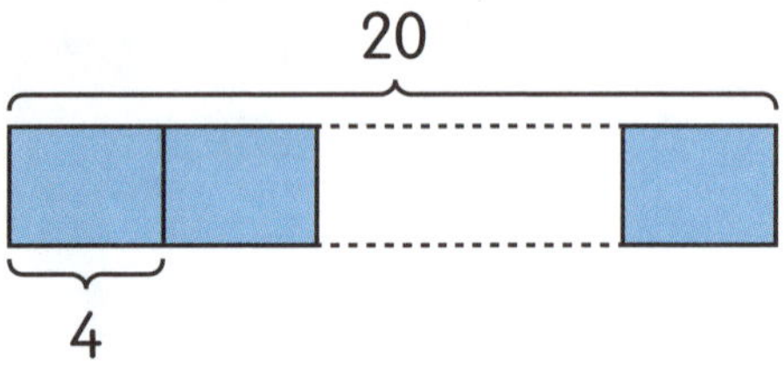

___ ÷ ___ = ___

Sally makes ___ picture frames altogether.

Practice Book 2B, pp.53 and 57

Unit 8

Length

Let's Learn!

Measuring in metres

1 Peter, Tai and Miya each have a metre ruler to measure the length of their tables.

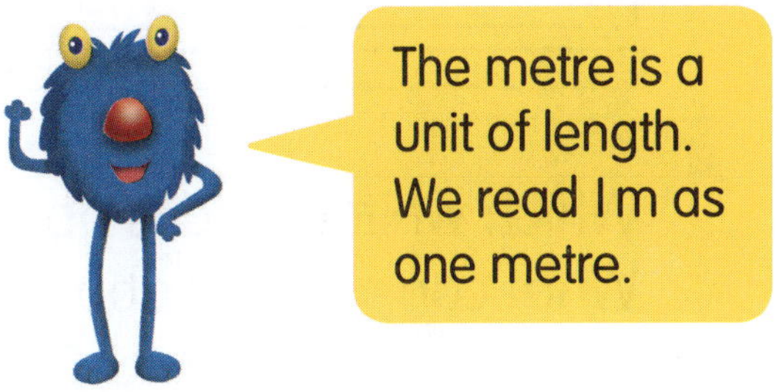

2

3 Metre rulers are placed along two whiteboards.

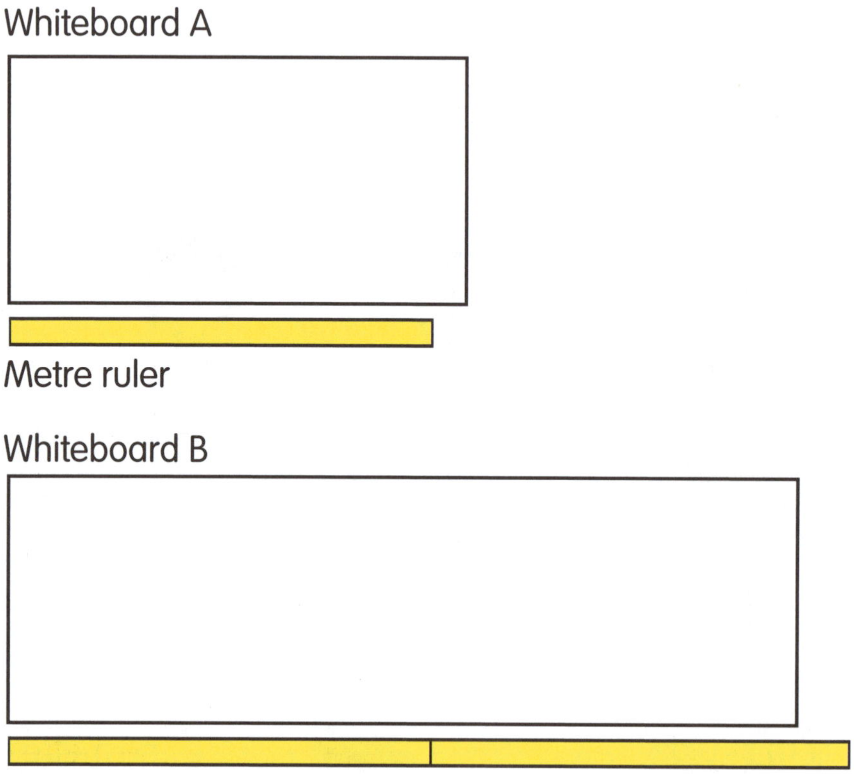

Which whiteboard is about 1 m long?
What can you say about the other whiteboard?

Say **more** or **less**.

a The length of whiteboard A is ______ than 1 m.

b The length of whiteboard B is ______ than 2 m.

4 Is the gate at your school more or less than 1 m high?

5 Name two objects in your school which are about 1 m long or 1 m high.

6 Name two objects in your house which are

a less than 1 m high **b** more than 1 m high

Activity

7 You will need a metre ruler or a piece of string that is 1 m long. First make a guess about the length or width of each object given below. Then use the ruler or string to measure each object.

		My guess	Actual length
a	The height of your classroom door.	**about 2 m**	**2 m**
b	The width of your classroom door.		
c	The width of your classroom window.		
d	The length of your friend's arm.		
e	The length of a table.		
f	The width of a shelf.		
g	The length of your classroom.		
h	The width of your classroom.		

Practice Book 2B, p.59

Let's Learn!

Comparing lengths in metres

1 Mrs Hill has an apple tree growing in her garden.
Mrs Cook also has an apple tree growing in her garden.
How can you find out which tree is taller?

Mrs Hill's apple tree

Mrs Cook's apple tree

2 A blue ribbon is 8 m long.

A red ribbon is 3 m long.

Which ribbon is longer?

How much longer?

Activity

3 **a** Use a metre ruler to answer these questions.
How long is the whiteboard in your classroom?
How long is the notice board in your classroom?
Which is longer, the whiteboard or the notice board?

b Choose two objects that can be found in your classroom.
Use a metre ruler to find out which of the two objects is longer.

4 Omar has two ropes.

Rope A is 24 m long.
Rope B is 42 m long.

Which rope is longer?
How much longer is it?

Practice Book 2B, p.63

Let's Learn!

Measuring in centimetres

1 This is a ruler.

The lunch box is 15 cm long.

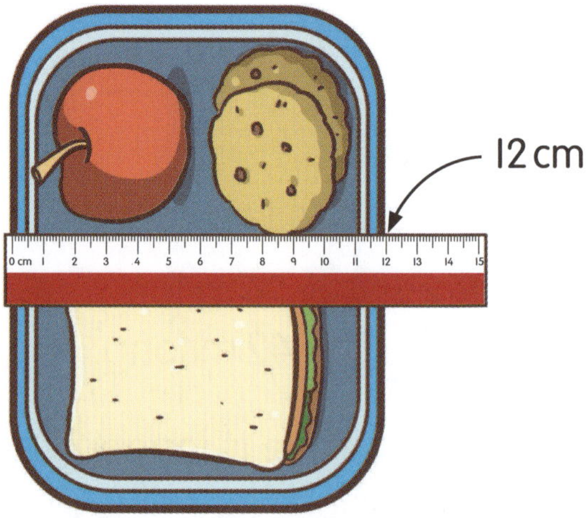

The lunch box is 12 cm wide.

2

The stack of books is 130 cm high.

3

The pencil case is

☐ cm long.

The pencil case is

☐ cm wide.

Activity 

4 Work in groups.

1 You will need two strips of paper each.

2 Measure the lengths of your strips.

3 Find out who else in the class has strips that are the same length as yours.

4 Order your strips. Begin with the shortest.

5 The shortest strip is ☐ cm long.

The longest strip is ☐ cm long.

5 Look at the lines below.
Measure each straight line with a ruler.
Use string to measure each curve.
Then place the string on a ruler to find its length in cm.

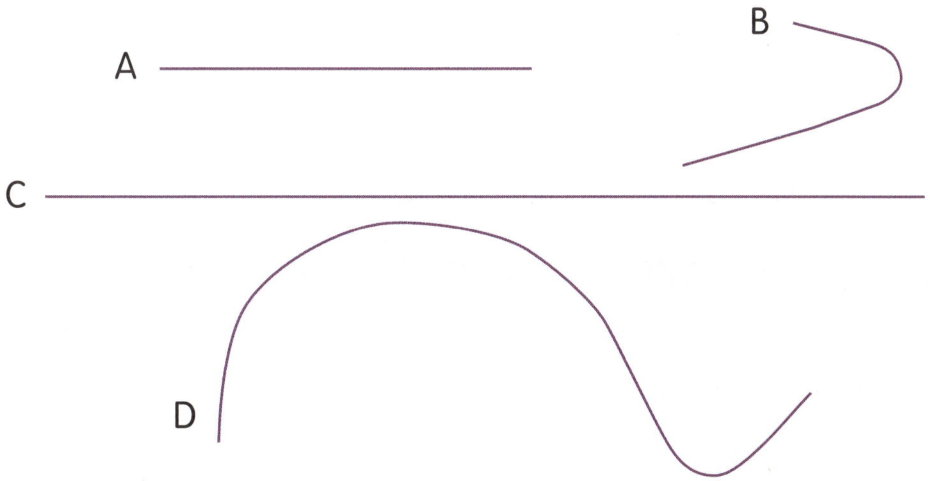

Which two lines have the same length?

6 What is the length of each line?
Use a ruler to find out.

a A ———————— B

b C ———————————— D

7 Draw a line 10 cm long.
Name it XY.

Draw a line 3 cm longer than XY.
Name it HK.

Draw a line 5 cm shorter than HK.
Name it MN.

What is the length of MN?

Practice Book 2B, p.65

Let's Learn!

Comparing lengths in centimetres

1

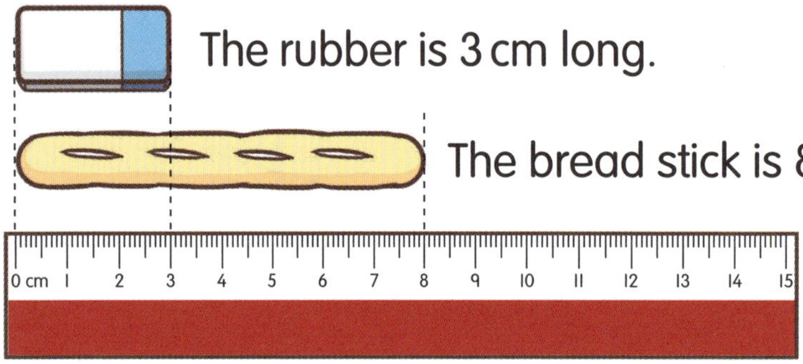

The rubber is 3 cm long.

The bread stick is 8 cm long.

The bread stick is longer than the rubber.

It is longer by 5 cm.

The rubber is shorter than the bread stick.

It is shorter by ☐ cm.

2

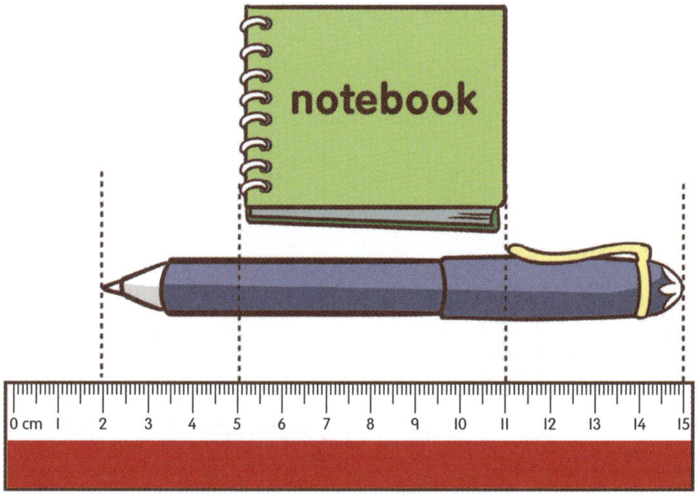

The pen is ☐ cm long.

The pen is ☐ than the notebook by ☐ cm.

3 Use a ruler to measure the lengths of these lines.

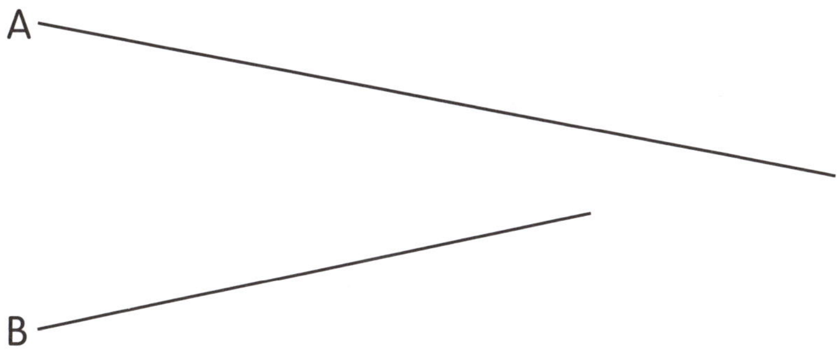

Line A = ☐ cm

Line B = ☐ cm

Line ☐ is longer than Line ☐.

How much longer? ☐ cm

Activity

4 You will need a picture frame.

1 Find the length around the picture frame.

2 Find another object and measure its length.
Is its length longer or shorter than the length around the picture frame?
By how much is it longer or shorter?

3 Measure the lengths of two other objects.
What is the length of the longer object?
How much longer is it?

Practice Book 2B, p. 67

Let's Learn!

Addition and subtraction of length

1 A cat walks 20 m in the morning and another 35 m in the evening.

a How far does the cat walk altogether?

b How much further does it walk in the evening?

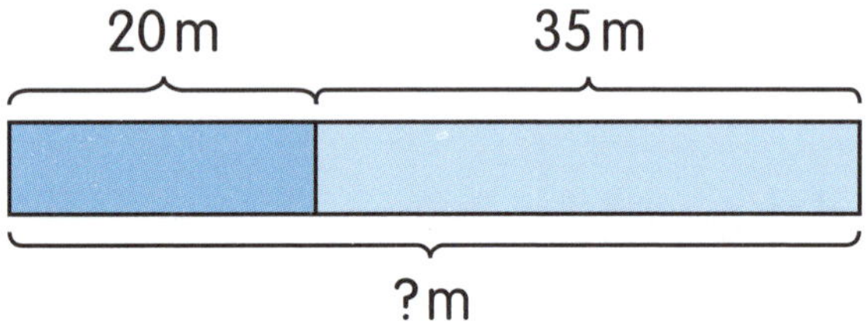

a 20 + 35 = 55
The cat walks 55 m altogether.

b 35 − 20 = 15
It walks 15 m further in the evening.

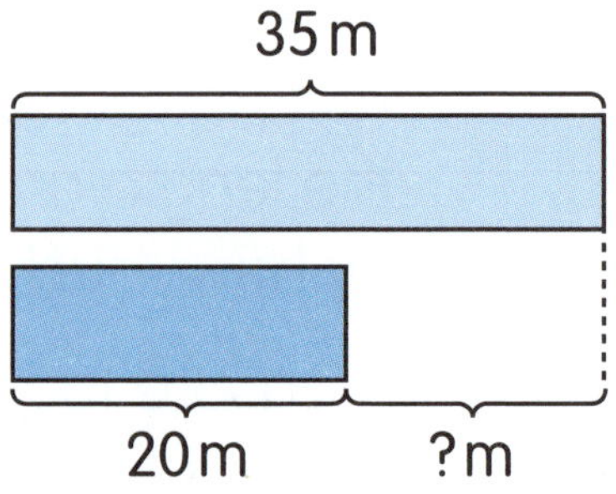

2

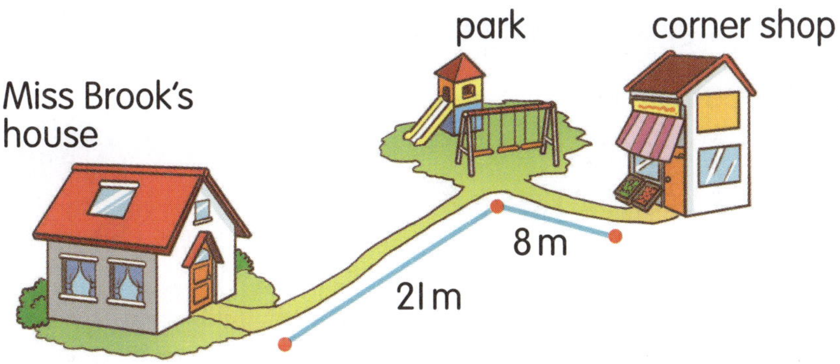

Miss Brook walks from her house to the corner shop to buy a drink.
On her way she passes the park.
How far does she walk?

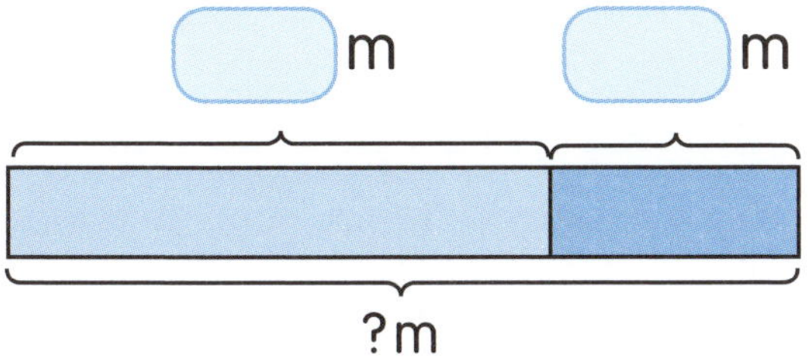

☐ + ☐ = ☐

She walks ☐ m altogether.

3

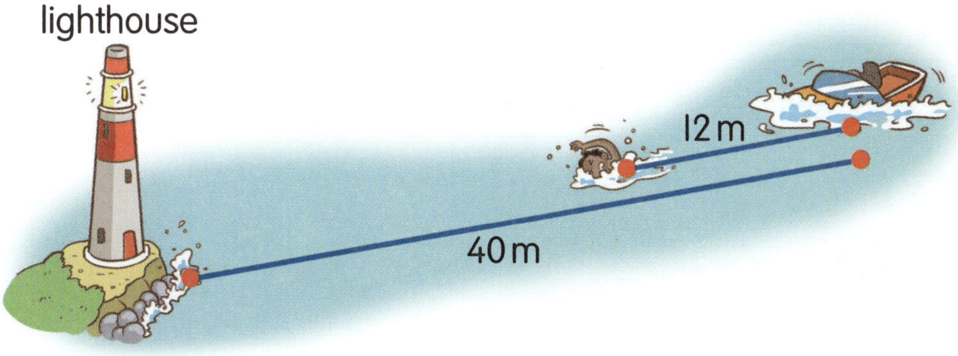

How far is the swimmer from the lighthouse?

☐ − ☐ = ☐

The swimmer is ☐ m from the lighthouse.

4 Millie has a piece of string. It is 45 cm long.
She cuts it into three pieces.
The first piece is 15 cm long.
The second piece is 12 cm long.

a Find the total length of the first and second pieces.

b What is the length of the third piece?

a

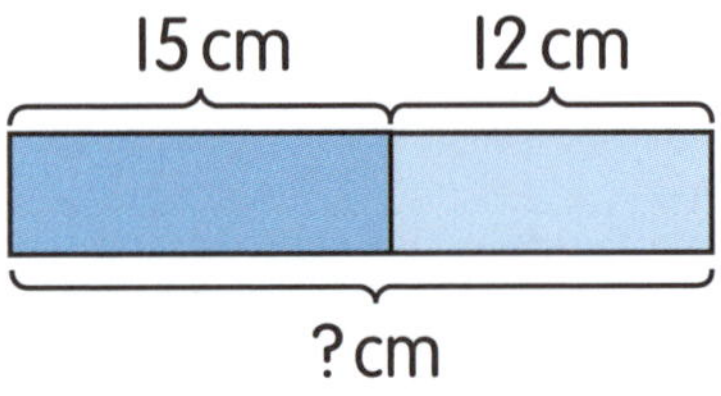

15 + 12 = 27

The total length of the first and second pieces is 27 cm.

b

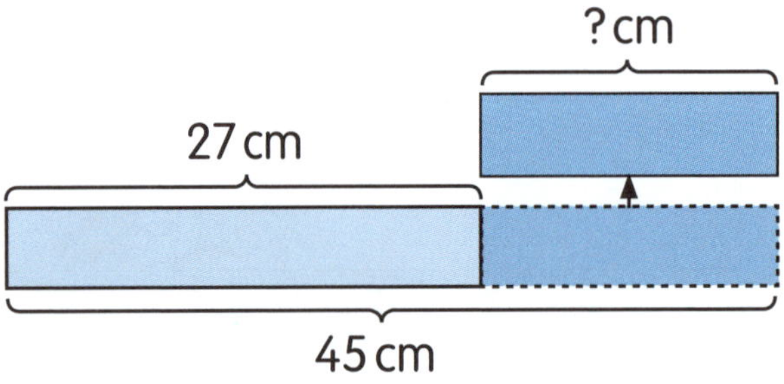

45 – 27 = 18

The length of the third piece is 18 cm.

5 Jack has a piece of red string. It is 100 cm long.
He uses 36 cm of string.
Then he joins a blue ribbon that is 75 cm long to his remaining red string.

What is the total length he makes in the end?

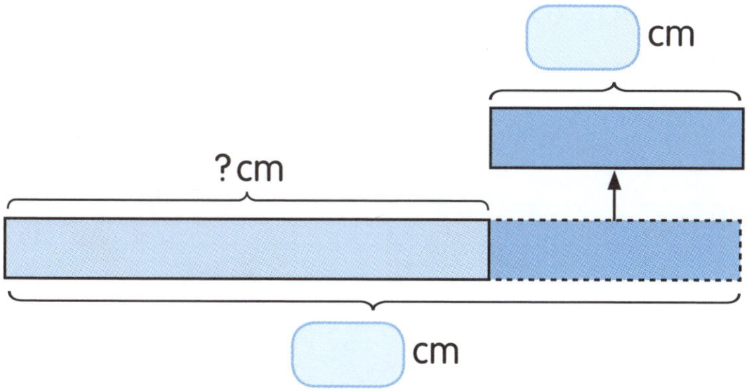

☐ – ☐ = ☐

The length of the red string he has left is ☐ cm.

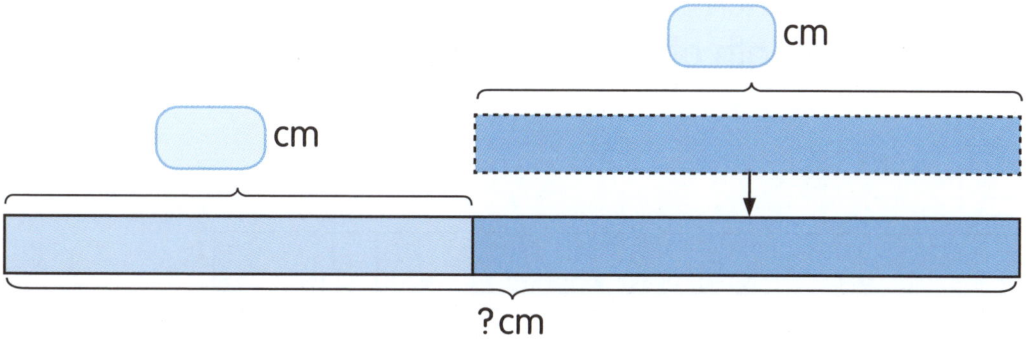

☐ + ☐ = ☐

The total length he makes in the end is ☐ cm.

Practice Book 2B, p.71

Let's Learn!

Multiplication and division of length

1 Jack has 4 coloured strips that are each 3 cm long.
He sticks them side by side to make a long strip.
How long is the strip?

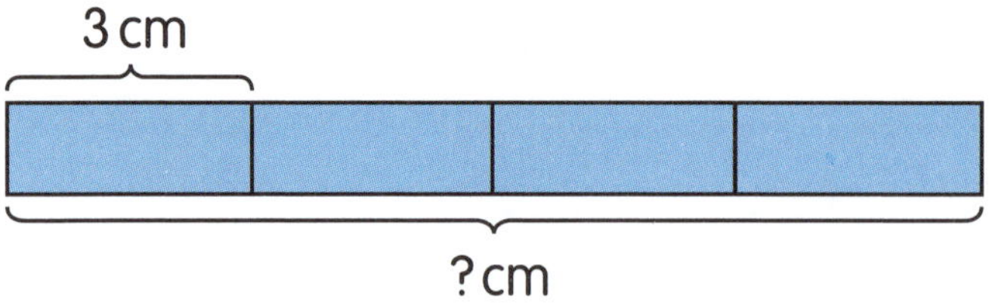

$4 \times 3 = 12$

The strip is 12 cm long.

2 Peter lays 5 building blocks along a wall.
The length of each building block is 10 cm.
What is the length of the 5 building blocks?

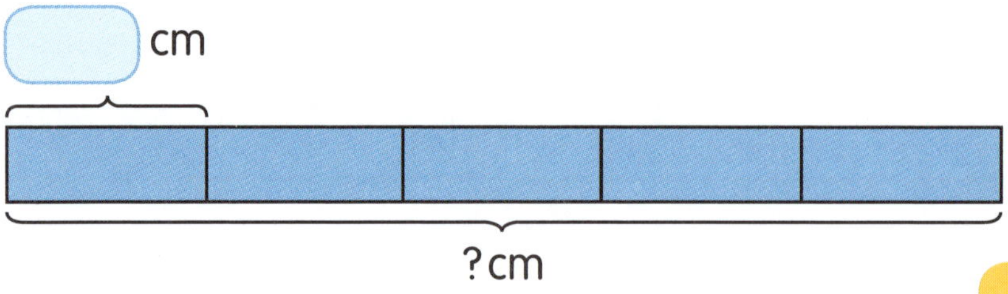

___ ◯ ___ = ___

The length of the 5 building blocks is ___ cm.

3 Farha has 3 boxes of the same size.
She arranges the boxes in a row.
Then she measures the length of the row of boxes.
It is 18 cm long.
What is the length of each box?

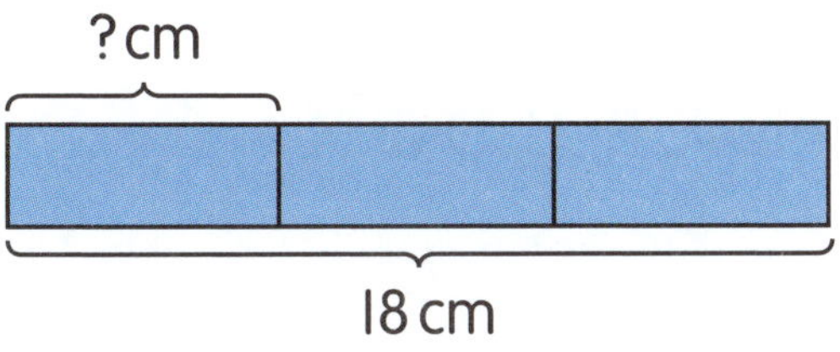

$18 \div 3 = 6$

The length of each box is 6 cm.

4 Mrs Brown has a ribbon 20 cm long.
She cuts it into a few pieces.
Each piece is 5 cm long.
How many pieces does Mrs Brown cut the ribbon into?

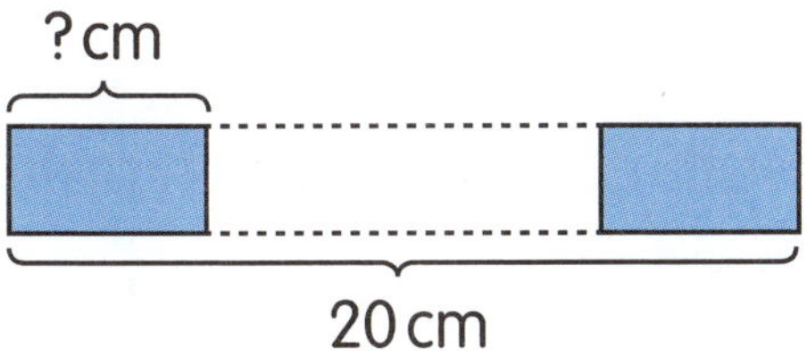

____ ○ ____ = ____

Mrs Brown cuts the ribbon into ____ pieces.

Practice Book 2B, p.77

Put On Your Thinking Caps!

5 An ant needs to find its way home.
It wants to find its way from A to C.
It can't pass through the points A, B, C, D or X more than once.

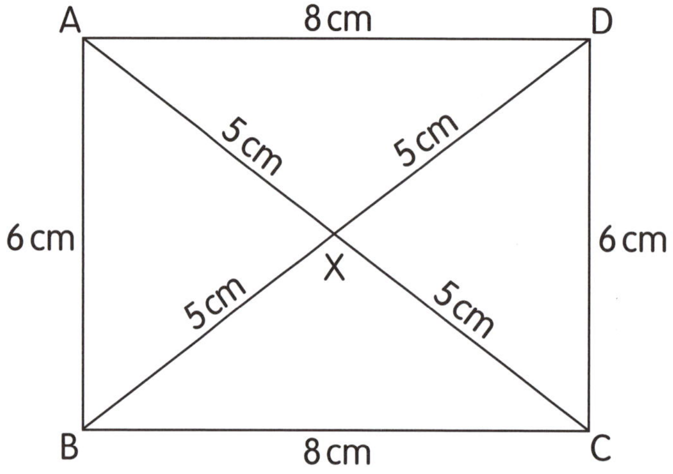

a The ant has travelled a length of 14 cm when it reaches C.
Which are the two paths it might have travelled?

b If the ant has travelled a length of 22 cm, which path has the ant taken?

c If the ant has travelled a length of 26 cm, which path has the ant taken?

d Find another path that the ant could have taken.
Write down the path.
Is there another path that has the same length?

Practice Book 2B, p.79

Practice Book 2B, p.80

Unit 9

Mass

Let's Learn!

Measuring in kilograms

1 Take a 1 kg weight.

1 Hold the 1 kg weight in your hand.

2 Next hold a pear, apple or any other fruit in your other hand.
Which is heavier, the 1 kg weight or the fruit?

3 Put the fruit down.
Pick up your school bag.
Which is heavier, the 1 kg weight or the school bag?

2

The bag of flour is **as heavy as** 1 kg.

3

The mass of the box of tissues is **less than** 1 kg.

4

What can you say about the mass of the box of cereal?

The mass of the box of cereal is **more than** 1 kg.

Activity

5 You will need some objects and a kitchen scale.

1 Estimate the mass of each object.
Is it 1 kg, less than 1 kg or more than 1 kg?
Record your estimates in a chart.

Name of object	My estimate			Actual mass		
	Less than 1 kg	1 kg	More than 1 kg	Less than 1 kg	1 kg	More than 1 kg
A packet of sugar						

2 Use the kitchen scale to find the mass of each object.
Copy and complete the chart.

3 How many of your estimates are correct?

Home Maths Ask your child to guess the masses of objects around the house. Encourage them to use a kitchen scale to find the actual mass. Note that at this point, your child is not expected to read the scale but to find if the object is 1 kg or is more/less than 1 kg.

6

The mass of the packet of sugar is 1 kg.

7

The mass of the bag of potatoes is ☐ kg.

8 Find the mass in kilograms.

a The mass of the bag of rice is ☐ kg.

b The mass of the bottle of juice is ☐ kg.

9 Find the mass in kilograms.

a

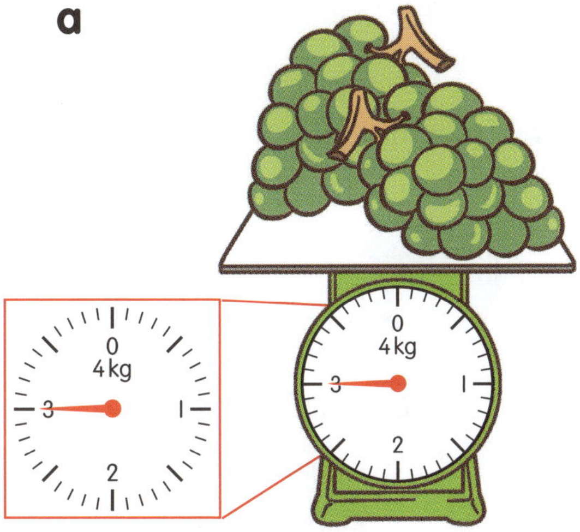

b

10

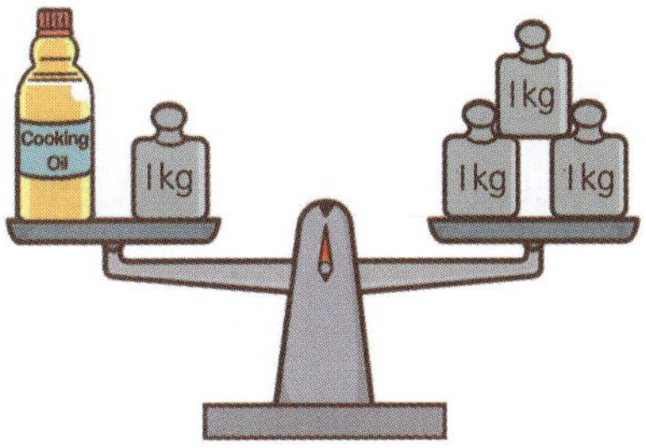

3 – 1 = 2

The mass of the bottle of oil is 2 kg.

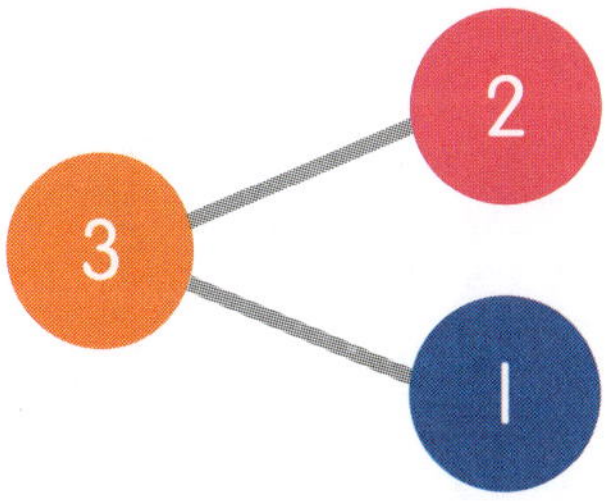

11

☐ – ☐ = ☐

The mass of the pineapple is ☐ kg.

Practice Book 2B, p.81

Let's Learn!

Comparing masses in kilograms

1

Parcel A

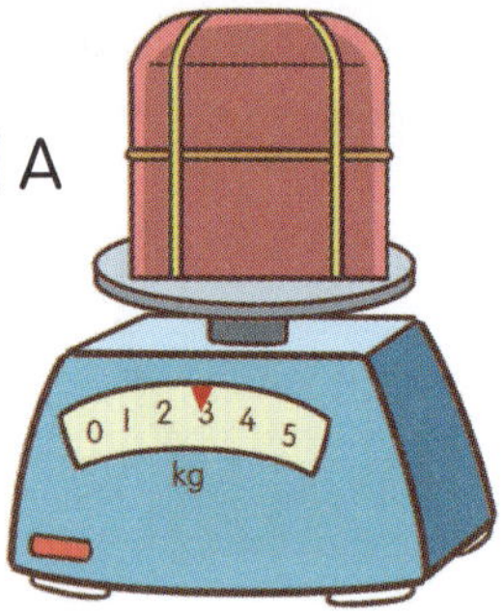

Parcel B

Parcel A has a mass of 3 kg. Parcel B has a mass of 2 kg.

Parcel A is heavier than Parcel B.

$3 - 2 = 1$

Parcel A is 1 kg heavier than Parcel B.

$3 + 2 = 5$

The total mass of Parcel A and Parcel B is 5 kg.

2

The mass of Parcel X is ____ kg.

The mass of Parcel Y is ____ kg.

Which parcel is heavier? ____

How much heavier? ____ kg

3

bag of carrots

bag of peppers

bag of cabbage

Which is the heaviest?

Which is the lightest?

Arrange them in order.

Begin with the lightest vegetables.

Do you think this picture is correct?

How do you know?

Practice Book 2B, p.83

Let's Learn!

Measuring in grams

1 We use smaller units to measure the mass of lighter objects.

These are some objects that are lighter than 1 kg.

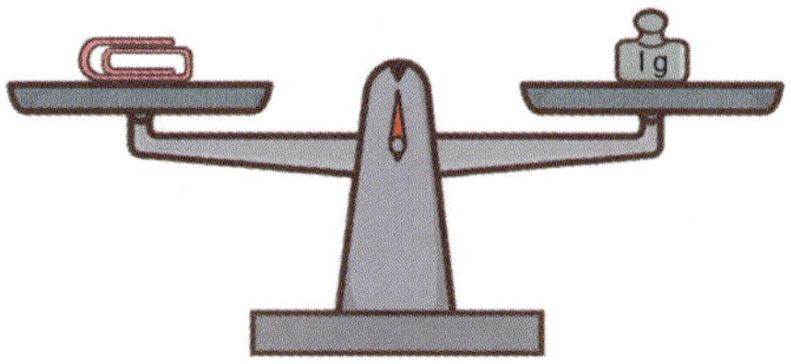

The paper clip has a mass of 1 g.

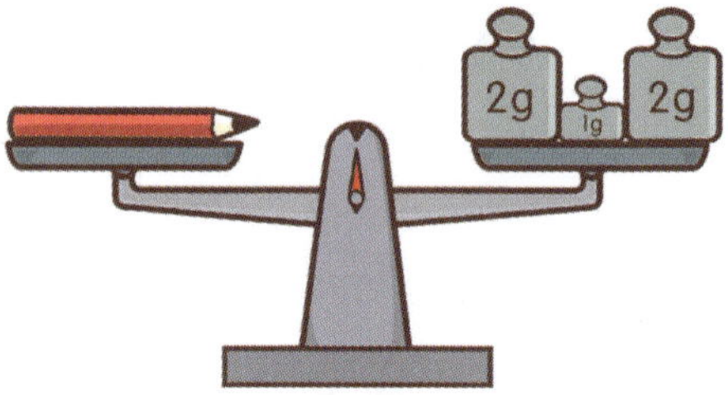

The pencil has a mass of 5 g.

2

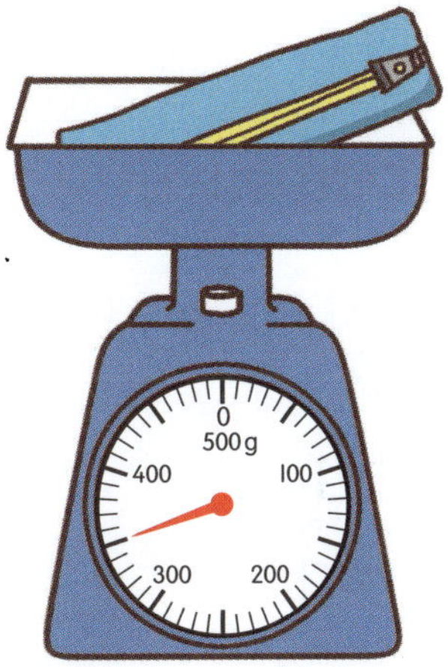

The pencil case has a mass of 350 g.

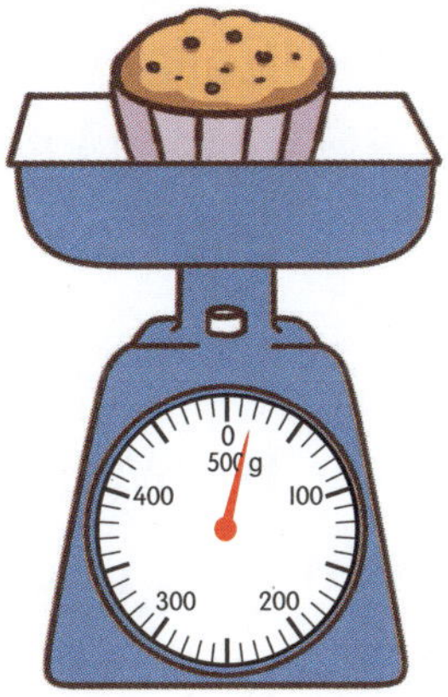

The muffin has a mass of 20 g.

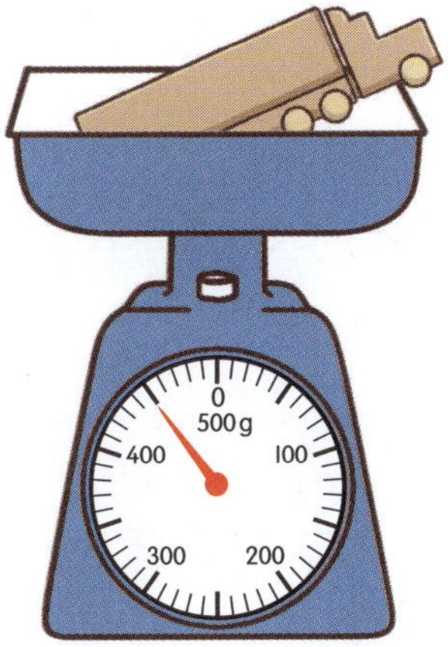

The toy truck has a mass of ☐ g.

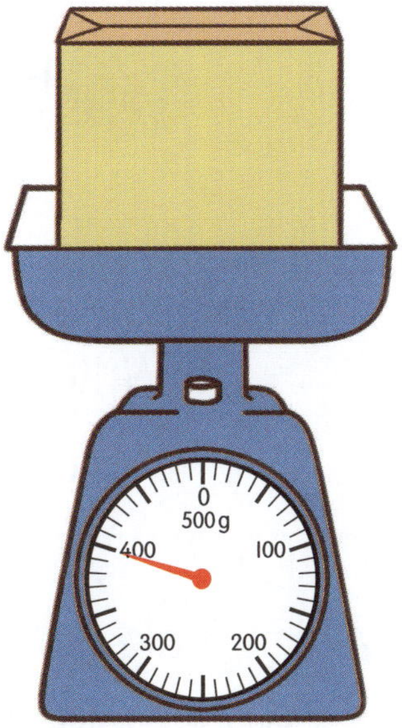

The parcel has a mass of ☐ g.

Home Maths

Try out a recipe with your child. Ask them to measure out the ingredients using a kitchen scale.

Activity

3 1 Collect objects from your classroom.
Use a kitchen scale to find their masses.
Put the objects into three groups.

a Masses between 50 g and 100 g.

b Masses between 100 g and 500 g.

c Masses between 500 g and 900 g.

2 Work in groups of three or four.
You will need some beans and a kitchen scale.

a Use the kitchen scale to weigh these amounts of beans:

50 g, 100 g, 150 g, 200 g, 250 g, 550 g, 750 g

b Put each amount in a paper bag.
Write the mass of the beans on each bag.

c Which bags add up to 1000 g?

4 Which scale would you use to find the mass of the

a watermelon?

b rubber?

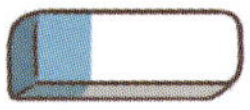

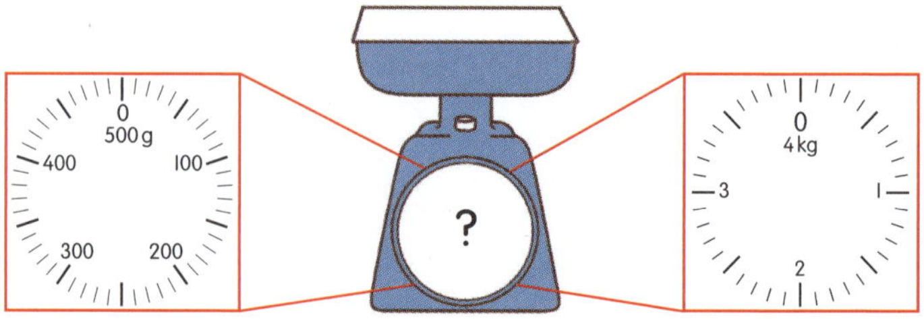

Scale A Scale B

Practice Book 2B, p.87

Let's Learn!

Comparing masses in grams

1

Jack is finding out the masses of his hole punch, stapler and book using a kitchen scale.

a This is what Jack writes on a piece of paper:

> The mass of my hole punch is 320 g.
>
> The mass of my stapler is 100 g.
>
> The mass of my book is 250 g.
>
> The lightest object is my stapler.
>
> The heaviest object is my hole punch.

b Copy and complete the following.

Use **lighter** or **heavier**.

The book is ______ than the stapler.

The stapler is ______ than the hole punch.

The hole punch is ______ than the total mass of the stapler and the book.

Activity

2 You will need three bags of marbles labelled X, Y and Z.

1 Hold each bag and guess how heavy it is.

2 Record your guesses in a chart.

3 Use a kitchen scale to find the actual masses. Record them in the chart.

	My guess	Actual mass
Bag X		
Bag Y		
Bag Z		

4 Copy and complete these sentences.

The heaviest bag has a mass of ___ g.

The lightest bag has a mass of ___ g.

Home Maths Put some small items (for example, marbles or beans) into 3 bags and ask your child to guess how heavy each bag is. Use a kitchen scale to find the actual mass.

3

a The mass of the tomato is 80 g.

b 450 – 80 = 370
The mass of the pumpkin is 370 g.

c The pumpkin is heavier than the tomato.

d 370 – 80 = 290
The pumpkin is 290 g heavier than the tomato.
The tomato is 290 g lighter than the pumpkin.

4

a What is the mass of the yoghurt pot?

b What is the mass of the box of cereal?

c Which is heavier?
How much heavier?

Activity

5

1 You will need an apple, an orange and another fruit.

2 Put only the apple and the orange on the scale. What is the mass of the apple and the orange together?

3 Remove the orange. What is the mass of the apple? Now find the mass of the orange.

4 Place the three fruits on the scale. What is the mass of all three together? Find the mass of the third fruit.

Practice Book 2B, p.93

Let's Learn!

Addition and subtraction of mass

1

Hardeep Millie Jack

What is the mass that Millie can carry?

$2 + 10 = 12$

Millie can carry 12 kg.

How much less mass can Hardeep carry than Jack?

$9 - 2 = 7$

Hardeep can carry 7 kg less than Jack.

2 Mr Hill's mass is 78 kg.
Mr Green's is 12 kg lighter than Mr Hill.
What is Mr Green's mass?

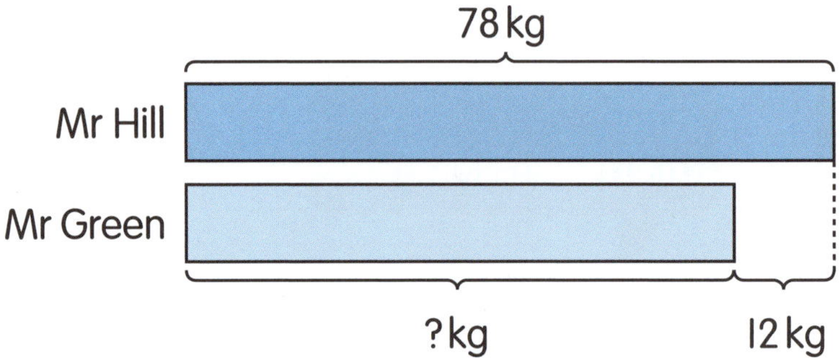

□ ○ □ = □

Mr Green's mass is □ kg.

3 The mass of the knight in armour is 80 kg.
The mass of the knight without the armour is 61 kg.
What is the mass of the armour?

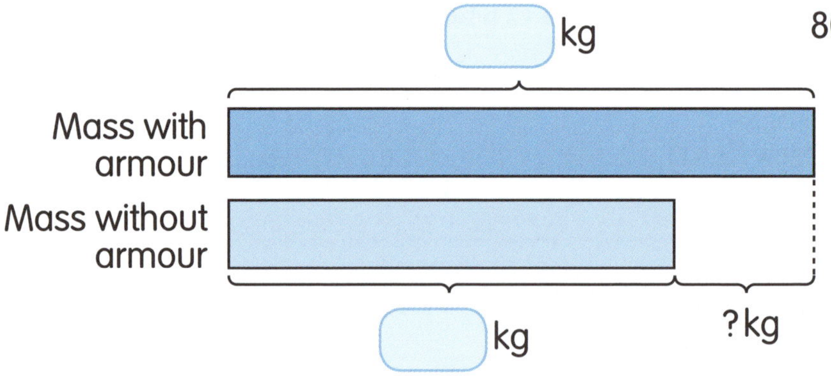

□ ○ □ = □

The mass of the armour is □ kg.

Activity

4

Name	Omar	Miya	Jack	Farha	Peter
Mass	29 kg	34 kg	22 kg	32 kg	20 kg

Each child picks apples at an orchard. Think of four questions you can ask using the masses.
Use the chart to answer the questions.

Example

a How much heavier is Farha's box of apples than Peter's?

b Add all the masses that are less than 30 kg.

c Omar's box is lighter than Miya's box by ☐ kg.

d What is the mass of both Omar's box and Miya's box?

5 The mass of a packet of sugar is 950 g.
Tai uses 250 g on Monday to bake some cakes.
He uses 180 g on Tuesday to bake some cookies.

a How much sugar did Tai use altogether?

b How much sugar is left at the end of Tuesday?

a 250 + 180 = 430
Tai uses 430 g of sugar altogether.

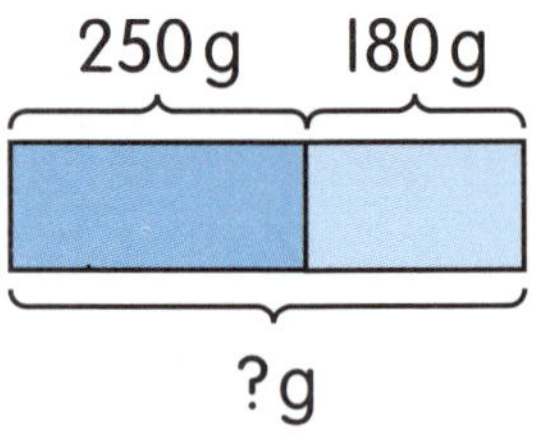

b

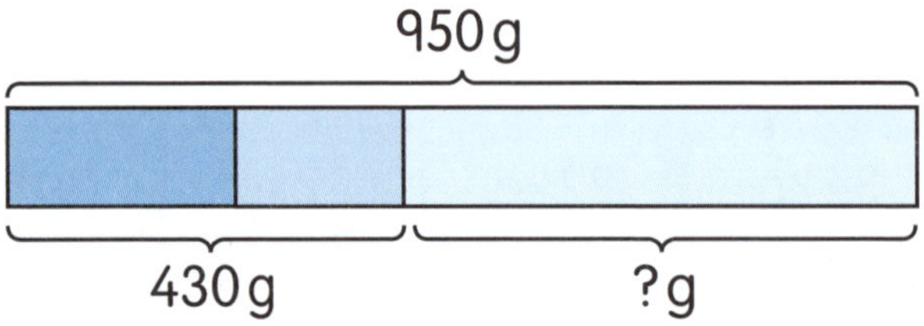

950 – 430 = 520
520 g of sugar is left at the end of Tuesday.

6 A garden centre has 88 kg of compost in stock.
It sells 32 kg on Monday and 19 kg on Tuesday.
How much compost does the garden centre have left at the end of Tuesday?

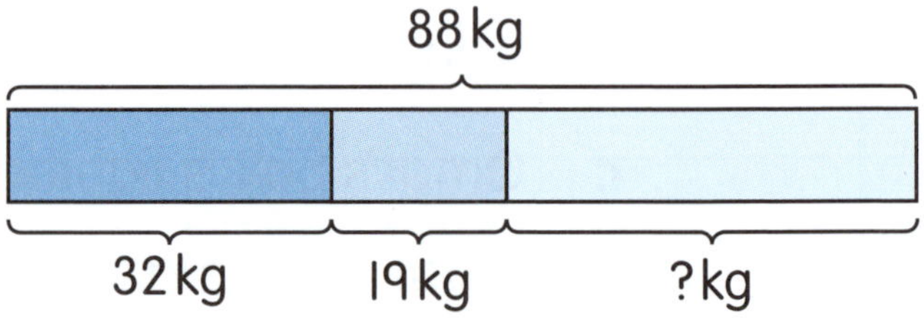

☐ ○ ☐ = ☐

The garden centre sells ☐ kg of compost altogether on Monday and Tuesday.

☐ ○ ☐ = ☐

The garden centre has ☐ kg of compost left at the end of Tuesday.

Practice Book 2B, p.95

Let's Learn! 

Multiplication and division of mass

1 Hardeep buys 5 bags of flour.
The mass of each bag of flour is 4 kg.
What is the mass of the 5 bags of flour?

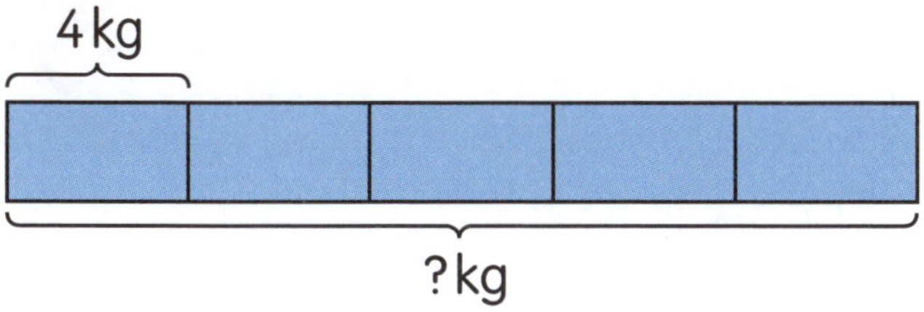

$5 \times 4 = 20$

The mass of the 5 bags of flour is 20 kg.

2 Farha has 3 bracelets.
The mass of each bracelet is 9 g.
What is the mass of the 3 bracelets?

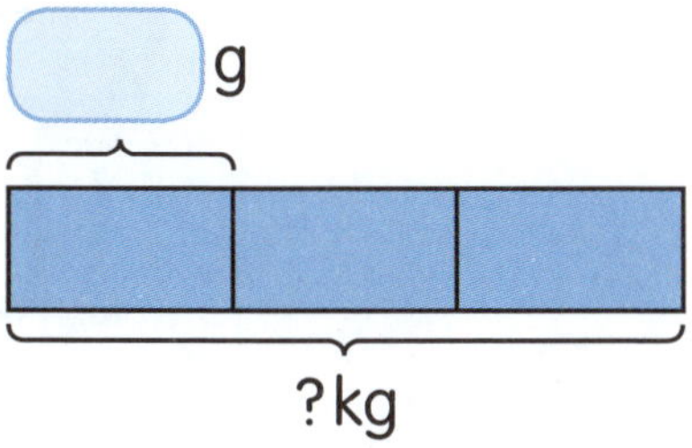

____ ____ ____ = ____

The mass of the 3 bracelets is ____ g.

3 Omar buys 3 bags of pears.
The mass of the 3 bags of pears is 24 kg.
Each bag has the same mass.
What is the mass of each bag of pears?

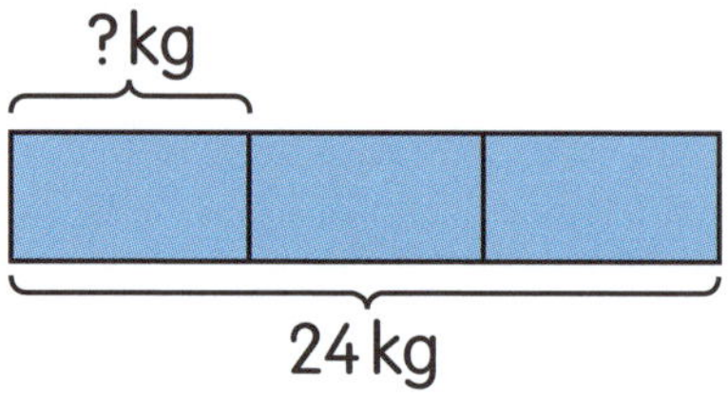

$24 \div 3 = 8$

The mass of each bag of pears is 8 kg.

4 The mass of 5 bags of sand is 30 kg.
Each bag of sand has the same mass.
What is the mass of each bag of sand?

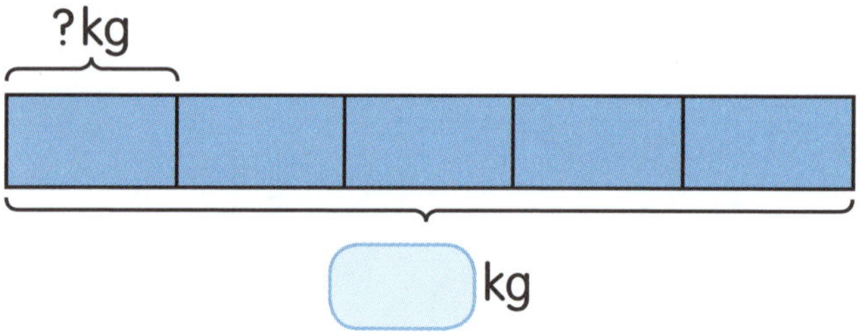

☐ ÷ ☐ = ☐

The mass of each bag of sand is ☐ kg.

5 Mr King bought some bags of potatoes.
The total mass of the potatoes was 36 kg.
Each bag of potatoes had a mass of 4 kg.
How many bags of potatoes did Mr King buy?

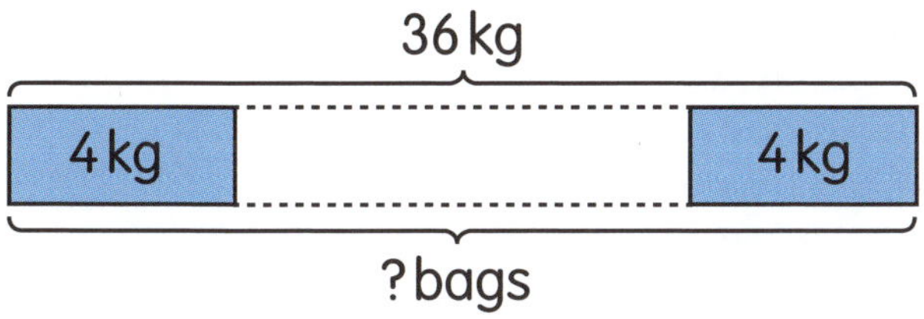

☐ ÷ ☐ = ☐

Mr King bought ☐ bags of potatoes.

Practice Book 2B, p.97

Put On Your Thinking Caps!

6

a Which box is heavier?

b How much heavier?

Practice Book 2B, p.99

Published by Marshall Cavendish Education
Times Centre, 1 New Industrial Road, Singapore 536196
Customer Service Hotline: (65) 6213 9444
Email: tmesales@mceducation.com
Website: www.mceducation.com

Distributed by
Oxford University Press
Great Clarendon Street, Oxford,
OX2 6DP, United Kingdom
www.oxfordprimary.co.uk
www.oxfordowl.co.uk

First published 2015
Reprinted 2015

ISBN 978-981-01-8868-9

Printed in China

Acknowledgements
Written by Dr Fong Ho Kheong, Chelvi Ramakrishnan and Michelle Choo

UK consultants: Carole Skinner, Simon d'Angelo and Elizabeth Gibbs

Cover artwork by Daron Parton

The authors and publisher would like to thank all schools and individuals who helped to trial and review Inspire Maths resources.